Improving Academic English

Clive Langham

Asahi Press

音声再生アプリ「リスニング・トレーナー」を使った 音声ダウンロード

朝日出版社開発のアプリ、「リスニング・トレーナー（リストレ）」を使えば、教科書の音声を スマホ、タブレットに簡単にダウンロードできます。どうぞご活用ください。

◉ アプリ【リスニング・トレーナー】の使い方

《アプリのダウンロード》

App Store または Google Play から 「リスニング・トレーナー」のアプリ （無料）をダウンロード

App Storeは こちら▶

Google Playは こちら▶

《アプリの使い方》

①アプリを開き「コンテンツを追加」をタップ
②画面上部に【 15702 】を入力しDoneをタップ

音声ストリーミング配信 》》》

この教科書の音声は、 右記ウェブサイトにて 無料で配信しています。

 https://text.asahipress.com/free/english/

Preface

This is the third book in the series on Academic English. It follows on from Developing Academic English and is entitled Improving Academic English. This book is aimed at people who are focusing on academic English skills. It will also be of interest to people taking tests such as TOEIC, TOEFL and IELTS, those thinking of studying overseas, and those who need academic English in the work place.

This book contains a total of 14 units that deal with current issues. Topics cover a wide range including the following; food waste, digital nomads, how to improve indoor air quality, lifestyle diseases, renewable energy, and smart cities. Reading passages in this book have an average of 650 words and in each unit about 15 keywords are introduced. These will help you to improve the range of your academic English vocabulary. There are a number of comprehension exercises that can be completed at home or in the classroom. Speaking activities are longer than those in books 1 and 2, and will help you to enhance your ability to talk about various topics. Each unit includes a short writing activity that is based on the unit topic. Finally, there is a research question that gives you the opportunity to do some research on the unit topic and write freely on an aspect of the topic that interests you.

As this is the last book in this series, I would like to wish readers the best of luck with their further studies of academic English. I hope that you will be able to put your knowledge of academic English to good use in your studies, professional life, and job.

Clive Langham

Contents

Improving Academic English

Food waste

In most countries, food is abundant and there is a tendency to take it for granted. However, the situation is changing and food sustainability is becoming a serious issue. The food supply in some countries is under threat from climate change. As temperatures go up and rainfall patterns become unstable, it is difficult to grow crops and, in some cases, yields have 5 declined significantly. The situation is made worse by the fact that the world's population is increasing. It is estimated that by the year 2050, the population will be over 9 billion people. In order to feed all of these people, food production must increase by 70 percent. This is a major challenge throughout the world. 10

It is of crucial importance to ensure a global sustainable food supply. Governments, organizations, and scientists are working on ways of making sure that there is a stable supply of food, and that everyone has enough to eat. Scientists are using genetic modification techniques to produce crops that are heat and drought resistant. A lot of progress has been made, but further 15 research and development is necessary.

A serious issue that remains to be addressed is food waste. In the region of 30 to 40 percent of all food is wasted. In the journey from a farm to a kitchen table, there are several stages. Food is wasted during the manufacturing process, in shops, supermarkets, restaurants, and in the home. 20 More than half of all food waste is in the home. This is a problem that we can control, but currently the issue is not receiving enough attention. The average amount of food wasted per day in homes in Western countries is around 1.96 kilos. About 40 percent of food wasted in the home is thrown away because it has not been used in time. This is food that is no longer fresh and is probably past the use-by date. About 25 percent of food wasted at home is due to people preparing, cooking, or serving too much. If we are more careful about these problems, food waste can be eliminated.

By changing our habits at home, we can reduce food waste and save money. Here are some useful tips for reducing food waste.

Always check what is in your refrigerator before you go shopping. This will stop you from buying anything that you do not need.

Planning meals carefully is important and will help you to avoid buying unnecessary food.

Before you go shopping, always make a list of what you need. If necessary, check your meal plans. Once you are in the supermarket, do not buy anything that is not on the list.

Do not buy too much. Supermarkets often have special offers such as buy two for the price of one. These offers look like a good deal, but they encourage you to buy too much. In many cases, you will end up throwing food away.

Most supermarkets will have a section for ugly fruits and vegetables that are the wrong shape or color. Make sure that you check these sections. You will find some bargains. You can save money and reduce food waste at the same time.

There are many ways to reduce food waste at home, and it is possible to make some big differences that will help you and the environment. It is always worth keeping in mind the idiom 'waste not, want not'. This means that if you do not use too much of something now, you will have enough later when you need it. The Japanese expression 'mottainai', which roughly translated means 'Oh, what a waste!', is being used in countries outside Japan. It was used by the Kenyan environmentalist, Wangari Maathai, as a slogan in a campaign for environmental protection. The fight against food waste is going on worldwide.

Match the words

Match the words 1 – 15 with the answers a – o.

_____ 1. abundant	a. person involved in protecting the environment
_____ 2. sustainability	b. goods that are sold at cheap prices
_____ 3. threat	c. amount produced
_____ 4. crops	d. eradicate, do away with, get rid of
_____ 5. yield	e. ability to maintain/support a process continuously
_____ 6. crucial	f. to make sure, guarantee
_____ 7. ensure	g. a motto, phrase or expression used in marketing
_____ 8. drought	h. plants grown and harvested for profit
_____ 9. resistant	i. you can eat food until, and on this date
_____ 10. address	j. tolerant, can withstand
_____ 11. use-by date	k. severe lack of water
_____ 12. eliminate	l. occurring in a large amount
_____ 13. special offer	m. extremely important
_____ 14. slogan	n. handle, deal with
_____ 15. environmentalist	o. danger

Answer the questions

Read questions 1 – 10 and choose the best answer from a – j.

Paragraph 1

_____ 1. What threat is the food supply in some countries facing?

_____ 2. When will the world's population reach more than 9 billion people?

Paragraph 2

_____ 3. What are governments, organizations, and scientists working on?

_____ 4. What kind of crops are being produced?

Paragraph 3

_____ 5. Where does more than half of all food waste occur?

_____ 6. How much food a day is wasted in homes in Western countries?

Paragraph 4

_____ 7. How can you avoid buying unnecessary food?

_____ 8. If you want to find some bargains, which section of the supermarket should you check?

Paragraph 5

_____ 9. If you want to avoid food waste, which idiom should you keep in mind?

_____ 10. How did Wangari Maathai use the Japanese expression *mottainai*?

....

a. By planning meals carefully

b. By the year 2050

c. In the home

d. Waste not, want not

e. Around 1.96 kilos

f. As a slogan in a campaign for environmental protection

g. The section for ugly fruits and vegetables that are the wrong shape or color

h. Climate change

i. Crops that are heat and drought resistant

j. Ways of making sure that there is a stable supply of food, and that everyone has enough to eat

Check the facts

Are these statements true (T), false (F), or not given (NG) according to the information in the passage?

Paragraph 1

_____ 1. Most countries do not have enough food.

_____ 2. A 70 percent increase in food production will be possible before 2050.

Paragraph 2

_____ 3. Governments want to create stable food supplies.

_____ 4. Genetically modified plants can survive in very hot, dry conditions.

Paragraph 3

_____ 5. Less than half of all food waste is in the home.

_____ 6. Nearly 2 kilos of food a day is wasted in homes in Western countries.

Paragraph 4

_____ 7. A good idea is to take a photo of the contents of your fridge.

_____ 8. Special offers look like a good deal, but people tend to buy too much.

Paragraph 5

_____ 9. Reducing food waste at home makes no difference at all.

_____ 10. The Japanese expression *mottainai* is now used in other countries.

Choose the best headings

Paragraph 1

1. Due to climate change, it is getting difficult to grow enough crops
2. Even though the world's population is increasing, there will be enough food

Paragraph 2

1. Creating a stable food supply is an important goal
2. Scientists have completed research on heat resistant crops

Paragraph 3

1. The problem of food waste is declining
2. With more care, food waste in the home could be completely avoided

Paragraph 4

1. If we change what we do at home, we can reduce food waste and save money
2. Fruits and vegetables that are ugly should be avoided

Paragraph 5

1. Action we take at home has no effect on the fight against food waste
2. All over the world, people are taking action against food waste

Speaking

🔊 Talk about food waste.

A: Did you know that more than half of all food waste is in the home?

B: No, I didn't know that. It's a lot of food.

A: Yes, in Western countries, the average amount of food wasted in the home is almost two kilos a day.

B: That's terrible. Why do people waste so much food?

A: One big reason is that they throw away food that is past its use-by date.

B: I see. I guess people buy too much food, put it in the refrigerator, and forget about it.

A: That's right. We need to plan meals more carefully and only buy food we need.

B: If we all did that, there would be less food waste.

Writing

🔊 Write about food waste.

Example:

Food waste is a serious problem in the home. In the UK, the average adult wastes 498 grams of food a day. This means that people lose a lot of money. In one year, the average household wastes food worth 496 pounds. The main foods that contribute to food waste in the UK are potatoes, bread, milk, and ready meals.

....

....

....

....

....

Research question

What are the best ways to reduce food waste in the home?

Check the internet and get information about how to reduce food waste in the home.

Example:

About half of all food waste is in the home. Almost two kilos of food a day is wasted. When we waste food, we also lose money. Here are some examples of how to reduce food waste at home and save money.

1. Don't buy too much food.
2. Check use-by dates before you buy anything.
3. Plan your meals. Some people plan up to a week's meals in advance.
4. If you have any leftover vegetables, make them into a soup.
5. If you have any meals that have not been eaten, put them in the freezer.

Cultivated meat

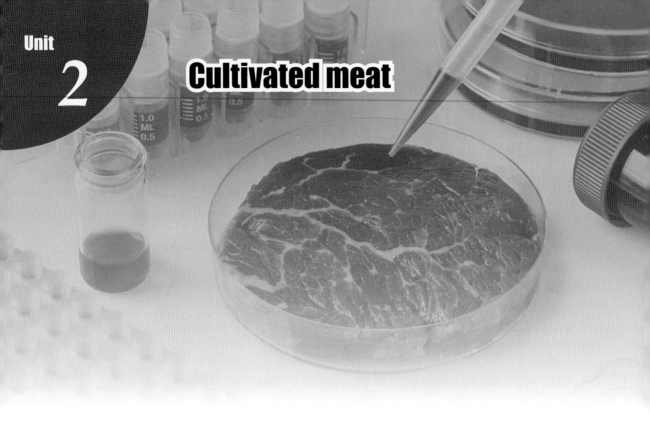

The number of people becoming vegetarians is increasing rapidly. The main reasons for this lifestyle change are as follows: eating a healthier diet, improving general health, reducing the risk of heart disease and cancer, losing weight, saving money, animal welfare, and concern about the environment. In recent years, people have become increasingly aware 5 of environmental issues and the fact that the meat industry is a major contributor to climate change. They think that if they stop eating meat, it will help to reduce greenhouse gas emissions. Let's look at how the meat and dairy industries have a negative effect on the environment.

You may be surprised, but raising animals for meat is responsible for 10 14.5 percent of the world's greenhouse gas emissions, which is the same as the CO_2 output of all cars, trucks, aircraft, and shipping combined. Another issue is that the meat and dairy industries cause deforestation, biodiversity loss, water pollution, and other environmental problems. It is a well-known fact that the Amazon rainforest is gradually being cut down and destroyed in 15 order to grow food for cattle and provide space for them to live. With global warming becoming an increasingly serious problem, governments have been considering how the negative effects of the meat and dairy industries can be reduced. Some countries, such as Denmark, have asked people to reduce the amount of meat that they eat. This means that the trend away from meat and 20 dairy products is rapidly increasing.

One possible solution to the problems caused by the meat industry is meat grown in a laboratory. Meat grown in this way is referred to as cultivated meat, lab-grown meat, and clean meat. Cultivated meat is grown from cells extracted from animals. Cells are placed in a bioreactor and grown to form tissue. What are the advantages of cultivated meat? In terms of environmental impact, it creates 92 percent less global warming, and 93 percent less air pollution than standard meat farming processes. It uses 95 percent less land, and 78 percent less water. Additionally, it is faster to produce cultivated meat than it is to produce meat using standard farming methods. For example, it takes in the region of seven weeks for a farmer to raise a flock of chickens, whereas a factory that produces cultivated meat can produce more meat in a much shorter time. There are other advantages as well. In the production of cultivated meat, it is possible to control the fat content of meat, which is important for health-conscious consumers. There are no antibiotics or bacteria in cultivated meat, which means that it is extremely clean and safe.

Although cultivated meat is still very new, several companies are now producing it, and have achieved good results. The first cultivated meat burger was made in 2013. It took two years to produce and had development costs of 330,000 US dollars. The current cost of such a burger is approximately 10 dollars. This means that the cost of making cultivated meat has dropped significantly in a relatively short time, but for the average consumer, it is too expensive. As the technology improves, the cost of cultivated meat will continue to fall, and this will make cultivated meat a more attractive product for consumers.

Another big issue is consumer reaction to cultured meat. Market research has shown that older people are uncomfortable about eating cultivated meat, and are reluctant to change their eating habits. For the younger generation, however, eating a hamburger from meat grown in a laboratory does not seem to be a problem. Some companies are responding to the above situation by experimenting with products that are a combination of cultivated meat and plant-based ingredients. This kind of hybrid burger could make the transition to 100 percent cultivated meat burgers easier and faster. Whatever happens, it is certain that laboratory-grown meat will be sold in restaurants and supermarkets in the near future, and that consumers will buy it.

Match the words

Match the words 1 – 13 with the answers a – m.

_____ 1. animal welfare

_____ 2. raising

_____ 3. greenhouse gas emissions

_____ 4. dairy industries

_____ 5. deforestation

_____ 6. biodiversity

_____ 7. extract

_____ 8. impact

_____ 9. antibiotics

_____ 10. bacteria

_____ 11. achieve

_____ 12. reluctant

_____ 13. transition

a. antimicrobial substances

b. removing forest so land can be used

c. unwilling to do something

d. effect, influence

e. take out, remove

f. get, obtain

g. to breed or grow animals or plants

h. biological variety and variability of life on Earth

i. process of changing from one condition to another

j. well-being of animals

k. business focusing on milk and milk products

l. gas emitted by human activities causing global warming

m. free-living organisms consisting of one biological cell

Answer the questions

Read questions 1 – 10 and choose the best answer from a – j.

Paragraph 1

_____ 1. What kind of problems are people becoming aware of?

_____ 2. What do people think will happen if they stop eating meat?

Paragraph 2

_____ 3. Why is the Amazon rainforest being cut down?

_____ 4. What did the Danish government ask people to do?

Paragraph 3

_____ 5. How long does it take to raise a flock of chickens?

_____ 6. Why is cultivated meat good for health-conscious consumers?

Paragraph 4

_____ 7. How long did it take to make the first cultured meat burger?

_____ 8. At the moment, how much does a cultivated meat burger cost?

Paragraph 5

_____ 9. What do we know about the reactions of older people to eating cultivated meat?

_____ 10. What is the reaction of younger people to eating cultivated meat?

a. About 10 dollars

b. Two years

c. Around 7 weeks

d. To grow food for cattle, and make space for them to live

e. Because the fat content of the meat can be controlled

f. They are uncomfortable about eating it

g. To reduce the amount of meat they eat

h. It does not seem to be a problem

i. Greenhouse gas emissions will go down

j. Environmental issues and the fact that the meat industry has a major role in causing climate change

Check the facts

Are these statements true (T), false (F), or not given (NG) according to the information in the passage?

Paragraph 1

_____ 1. The number of people becoming vegetarians has increased slowly.

_____ 2. The biggest reason for becoming a vegetarian is animal welfare.

Paragraph 2

_____ 3. Cars, trucks, aircraft, and shipping emit more CO_2 than raising animals for meat.

_____ 4. The Amazon rainforest is being cut down at a fast rate.

Paragraph 3

_____ 5. The environmental impact of cultivated meat is smaller than that of standard meat farming processes.

_____ 6. Cultivated meat is considered to be extremely clean and safe because it does not contain antibiotics or bacteria.

Paragraph 4

_____ 7. Cultivated meat burgers can be bought in most supermarkets.

_____ 8. The price of cultivated meat will go down as technology develops.

Paragraph 5

_____ 9. Older people are willing to alter their eating habits.

_____ 10. Special cultivated meat burgers have been produced for older people.

Choose the best headings

Paragraph 1

1. People are changing their lifestyle for a number of different reasons
2. The meat industry causes more damage to the environment than the dairy industry

Paragraph 2

1. The meat and dairy industries create a large number of environmental issues
2. People in only one country have been asked to give up eating meat completely

Paragraph 3

1. Cultivated meat has a number of significant advantages
2. Standard meat farming has less effect on the environment than any other farming methods

Paragraph 4

1. Results from companies producing cultured meat are not promising
2. As the price of cultivated meat goes down, it will become increasingly attractive to consumers

Paragraph 5

1. The majority of people cannot get used to cultivated meat
2. Hybrid burgers may make the move to cultivated meat easier and faster

Speaking

Talk about cultivated meat.

A: Do you eat a lot of meat?

B: No, I have given up eating meat completely.

A: Why is that?

B: There are too many problems associated with meat production.

A: What kind of things?

B: Meat production is bad for the environment and causes global warming.

A: But don't you miss eating meat?

B: No, I don't. You can buy hamburgers made of plant-based ingredients. They taste really good. Anyway, in a few years, we will all be eating meat grown in a laboratory. It is called cultivated meat.

Writing

Write about cultivated meat.

Example:

Cultivated meat is grown in a laboratory from cells extracted from animals. Meat grown in this way can be produced more quickly than meat produced using standard farming methods. It does not contain antibiotics or bacteria, and is extremely clean and safe. The fat content can be controlled, which is important for health-conscious consumers.

Research question

Why do people become vegetarians?

Check the internet and get information about why people become vegetarians.

Example:

In the US, there are roughly 16.4 million vegetarians, which is about 5 percent of the population. Younger people are more likely to be vegetarians. Here are some reasons why people choose to become vegetarians.

To reduce global warming.

To reduce the risk of heart disease.

To save money.

To lose weight.

Because they think it is wrong to kill and eat animals.

Unit 3

A frugal lifestyle

The word consumerism comes from the verb to consume, which means to use up resources or materials. Consumerism is a theory that spending money, and purchasing goods and services, benefits the economy. In today's society, it is clear that the majority of people create a life that focuses on money and buying things. In many cases, they buy too much. This means 5 that by the end of the month, they have almost no money left. It is said that 76 percent of Americans live paycheck to paycheck. With these kinds of spending habits, people go into debt, and money becomes a major source of stress and unhappiness.

Another problem with consumerism is that it puts pressure on natural 10 resources, and creates a large amount of waste as people dispose of unwanted things. This kind of lifestyle has a negative effect on the environment and is thought to contribute to climate change. The main negative effects of consumerism include wasting natural resources and pollution of the Earth. In other words, the mass consumption that is commonly seen today means 15 that we are overusing the Earth's natural resources. The problem is getting worse because the number of middle-class people is rapidly increasing as developing countries become more prosperous. As this happens, there will be more demand for energy, food, electronic appliances, cars and so on. All of this will put a massive burden on the Earth. 20

In recent years, however, there has been a slow but sure movement away from consumerism toward a more frugal lifestyle, where people are careful with money, avoid overspending, and try hard not to waste resources. The word frugal refers to the careful management of resources such as energy, food, time, money, and belongings. Synonyms for frugal are economical and thrifty. A frugal lifestyle is the opposite of consumerism and is gradually catching on with people around the world. This kind of lifestyle reduces demand for resources and makes people consider how to use resources sustainably.

Since the Covid-19 pandemic, there has been a significant shift toward less consumption and greater interest in frugality. During the pandemic, people reconsidered their lifestyles, spending, and shopping habits. People did not go out much, and concentrated on home activities. There was a boom in home cooking. People who had never really been interested in cooking started baking bread, and cooking meals from scratch. Some people took up practical hobbies such as sewing, knitting, making their own clothes, and doing small DIY projects. People learned new skills such as how to repair a bicycle or make soba noodles.

Another major shift in lifestyle during the pandemic was a movement away from buying new things to buying second-hand things. People bought second-hand clothes, furniture, and domestic appliances. The popularity of shops selling second-hand goods increased rapidly, and searching for used goods in shops, on the internet, and in flea markets became popular. The number of websites selling used goods increased. In fact, during the pandemic, the second-hand economy grew by nearly 20 percent.

One of the few positive things to emerge from the pandemic was the increase in the popularity of a frugal lifestyle. People are reducing their consumption, buying fewer things, and are happy to purchase used goods. Additionally, they have developed practical skills that save money and give them a sense of satisfaction. Frugality is now seen as a smart lifestyle choice that has fewer negative effects on the environment, and makes you happier. The movement has become more mainstream and events such as Buy Nothing Day, an international day of protest against consumerism, have helped to raise awareness of the benefits of a frugal lifestyle.

Match the words

Match the words 1 – 15 with the answers a – o.

____	1. consumerism	a.	words with a similar meaning
____	2. theory	b.	well-off, wealthy, rich
____	3. debt	c.	huge, gigantic, very big
____	4. contribute	d.	change
____	5. prosperous	e.	a heavy load or task
____	6. massive	f.	trend, tendency
____	7. burden	g.	from zero, from the beginning
____	8. frugal lifestyle	h.	belief, hypothesis, thesis
____	9. synonym	i.	money that is owed
____	10. catch on	j.	rethink, think again about something
____	11. shift	k.	come out
____	12. reconsider	l.	help to cause or bring about
____	13. from scratch	m.	become popular
____	14. emerge	n.	careful in the use of one's money and resources
____	15. movement	o.	idea that spending money and buying goods benefits the economy

Answer the questions

Read questions 1 – 12 and choose the best answer from a – l.

Paragraph 1

____ 1. For many people, what are the most important things in life?

____ 2. For people who spend too much, what usually happens by the end of the month?

Paragraph 2

____ 3. What are the main negative effects of consumerism?

____ 4. Why is the problem of overusing the Earth's natural resources getting worse?

Paragraph 3

____ 5. What has consumerism slowly moved toward?

____ 6. What are two synonyms for frugal?

Paragraph 4

____ 7. During the pandemic, what did people think about changing?

____ 8. What kind of home activity became very popular during the pandemic?

Paragraph 5

____ 9. Where did people look for second-hand items?

____ 10. By how much did the second-hand economy increase?

Paragraph 6

____ 11. After Covid-19, how did people see frugality?

____ 12. What did Buy Nothing Day raise awareness of?

----

a. As a smart lifestyle choice

b. Their lifestyles, spending, and shopping habits

c. Economical and thrifty

d. A more frugal lifestyle

e. Wasting natural resources and pollution of the Earth

f. The benefits of a frugal lifestyle

g. Home cooking

h. Focusing on money and buying things

i. Because the number of middle-class people is rapidly increasing as developing countries become more prosperous

j. By almost 20 percent

k. They have very little money left

l. In shops, on the internet, and in flea markets

Check the facts

Are these statements true (T), false (F), or not given (NG) according to the information in the passage?

Paragraph 1

_____ 1. For a minority of people, focusing on money and buying things is the most important thing in life.

_____ 2. People who spend too much money may end up in debt.

Paragraph 2

_____ 3. Consumerism is thought to bring about climate change.

_____ 4. Middle-class people in developing countries are getting poorer.

Paragraph 3

_____ 5. People who adopt a frugal lifestyle tend to live in rural areas.

_____ 6. A frugal lifestyle is slowly becoming popular with many people.

Paragraph 4

_____ 7. Home cooking became popular, particularly with people who had little experience of cooking.

_____ 8. People enjoyed having home parties with their friends.

Paragraph 5

_____ 9. Shops selling second-hand goods reduced their prices.

_____ 10. The second-hand economy increased to a value of 10 million USD.

Paragraph 6

_____ 11. After the pandemic, frugality became unpopular.

_____ 12. Buy Nothing Day is celebrated around the world.

Choose the best headings

Paragraph 1

1. For many people, the end of the month is a time when they have no money

2. Going into debt is not an issue for people

Paragraph 2

1. Consumerism has a positive impact on the environment

2. The increase in the number of middle-class people in developing countries will put more pressure on the Earth

Paragraph 3

1. There has been a steady shift from spending on things to a frugal lifestyle

2. Consumerism and a frugal lifestyle are both similar and becoming more popular

Paragraph 4

1. A negative aspect of Covid-19 was that many people reevaluated their lifestyles

2. During the pandemic, people engaged in practical activities and learned new skills

Paragraph 5

1. People who previously bought new things became interested in buying second-hand goods during the pandemic

2. Second-hand shops increased their sales by reducing prices

Paragraph 6

1. As a result of the pandemic fewer people became interested in frugal lifestyles

2. People have become more aware of frugal lifestyles due to the effect of events such as Buy Nothing Day

Speaking

Talk about frugal lifestyles.

A: I noticed that you have started bringing a lunchbox every day. Don't you eat out anymore at lunchtime?

B: No, I decided to adopt a more frugal lifestyle.

A: What do you mean?

B: Well, I'm more careful about how much money I spend nowadays. If I bring a lunchbox to work every day, I can save a lot of money.

A: I see. What else do you do to save money?

B: I have given up buying expensive clothes.

A: Don't you buy any clothes at all?

B: I buy fewer clothes. And I try to find used clothes. It saves a lot money and is better for the environment.

Writing

Write about frugal lifestyles.

Example:

Frugal people are careful with money, do not overspend, and avoid wasting resources. The number of people who adopt a frugal lifestyle is increasing. During the Covid-19 pandemic, a lot of people changed their lifestyle, spending, and shopping habits. People learned new practical skills such as how to bake bread and cook meals from scratch.

Research question

What are some common ways of living a frugal lifestyle?

Check the internet and get information about ways of living a frugal lifestyle.

Example:

The number of people who adopt a frugal lifestyle is going up. Here are some lifestyle choices that they make.

1. Shop at less expensive grocery stores
2. Eat at home and don't eat out or have takeouts
3. Buy used clothes
4. Collect discount coupons
5. Reduce the amount of energy used at home

Unit 4

Digital nomads

Are you familiar with the term 'digital nomad'? Digital nomads are usually freelancers who work remotely, using laptops and other mobile devices for their job. They work from hotels, coffee shops, public libraries, coworking spaces, and rental offices using Wi-Fi, smartphones, and computers to access the internet. Some digital nomads travel from place to 5 place in their home countries, others move from one country to another. In a survey carried out in 2020, almost 20 million Americans said they were digital nomads. This was twice as many as in 2019.

What do we know about the history of digital nomads? In 1964, Arthur C. Clarke, an English science fiction writer, predicted that in the future it would 10 be possible for people to work remotely from a place like Bali, Indonesia in the same way as they could work in London or New York. It is said that Steve Roberts was the first digital nomad. He cycled across the United States using a specially designed and computerized bicycle in 1983. In December 1997, Tsugio Makimoto and David Mannes published a book entitled Digital 15 Nomad, which focused on technology that would allow people to live and work while moving from place to place. This was the first time that the expression digital nomad appeared in print. It is not known if they were the first people to use the term or whether it was used previously.

A lot of people are attracted to the nomadic lifestyle because it gives 20 them the chance to travel to and work in exotic locations. Many digital nomads choose to work in places where the cost of living is low. Money that they earn by working online with clients in rich countries goes further than it would at home. This means that they can enjoy a higher standard of living in the country they are working in. Digital nomads like having freedom, the opportunity to travel and see new places, and being their own boss. They can choose to live in tropical countries where the weather is warm all year round. Working hours can be flexible and digital nomads get enough free time to enjoy themselves.

Some digital nomads spend several years in foreign countries, and face challenges such as language issues, communication problems, and culture shock. Some people feel isolated, and miss their friends and family back home. They also have difficulty making friends in the countries they are working in. Other problems are healthcare, taxes, work visas, stress, overwork, and burnout. In some cases, depending on where their clients are based, different time zones can be an issue, and digital nomads sometimes end up working early in the morning or late at night in order to be in contact with their clients.

Some countries are trying to attract digital nomads because they benefit the economy. In 2020, Estonia launched a new digital nomad visa. It is valid for one year and allows people to live and work in the country legally. In 2021, Croatia introduced a special digital nomad visa. The National Tourist Board campaign was called, 'Croatia, your new office'. Thailand and the United Arab Emirates have similar visas.

Here are some facts about digital nomads.

What kind of work do digital nomads do? The following jobs are popular: IT, marketing, e-commerce, designing websites, writing, translating, editing, teaching, and proofreading. It is not uncommon for people to do several of these jobs at the same time in order to make a living.

Who are digital nomads? The average digital nomad is 35 years old. Thirty-one percent of them are from the US. Forty-nine percent are female and fifty-one percent are male.

What are the most popular locations for digital nomads to work in? The top 5 most popular countries are Mexico (14%), Thailand (12%), Indonesia (9%), Colombia (7%), and Vietnam (5%).

How many digital nomads are there? Although it is difficult to get accurate information on the number of digital nomads, there are thought to be over 35 million around the world. This number is increasing all the time.

Match the words

Match the words 1 – 12 with the answers a – l.

____	1. digital nomad	a.	forecast, tell in advance
____	2. work remotely	b.	word or expression
____	3. mobile devices	c.	start or set in motion an activity
____	4. predict	d.	to be away from your normal work place
____	5. term	e.	can be used for a fixed period of time
____	6. nomadic lifestyle	f.	business that is conducted online
____	7. exotic location	g.	lifestyle of moving from one place to another
____	8. communication problem	h.	physical or mental breakdown due to stress
		i.	tropical islands in Asia or South America
____	9. burnout	j.	handheld computers, smartphones or tablets
____	10. launch	k.	a person working remotely and moving a lot
____	11. valid	l.	difficulties understanding what other people
____	12. e-commerce		say

Answer the questions

Read questions 1 – 12 and choose the best answer from a – l.

Paragraph 1

____ 1. What are digital nomads?

____ 2. In 2019, how many digital nomads were there?

Paragraph 2

____ 3. Who was the first digital nomad?

____ 4. When did the term digital nomad first appear in books and newspapers?

Paragraph 3

____ 5. What kind of countries do digital nomads like to work in?

____ 6. What do we know about the working hours of digital nomads?

Paragraph 4

_____ 7. What kind of problems do digital nomads face?

_____ 8. Why do digital nomads have to work early in the morning or late at night?

Paragraph 5

_____ 9. Why do some countries welcome digital nomads?

_____ 10. How long does the digital nomad visa launched in Estonia last?

Paragraph 6

_____ 11. Which is the most popular country to work in?

_____ 12. What is the total number of digital nomads?

a. Places with a low cost of living

b. For a year

c. Because they help the economy

d. Steve Roberts

e. Because their clients are based in different time zones

f. In 1997

g. Language problems, culture shock, and loneliness

h. 10 million

i. They are flexible

j. People who work for themselves in various locations using mobile devices

k. Mexico

l. Over 35 million worldwide

Check the facts

Are these statements true (T), false (F), or not given (NG) according to the information in the passage?

Paragraph 1

_____ 1. The number of digital nomads has remained the same for several years.

_____ 2. Some companies are encouraging their staff to work in rental offices.

Paragraph 2

_____ 3. The trend toward working remotely was predicted in 1964.

_____ 4. A book published in 1997 focused on the working lives of digital nomads.

Paragraph 3

_____ 5. One of the attractions of being a digital nomad is the opportunity to have a better standard of living.

_____ 6. Digital nomads have to follow orders from their managers.

Paragraph 4

_____ 7. Due to various problems, a lot of digital nomads soon return to their home countries.

_____ 8. Digital nomads sometimes suffer from mental problems caused by stress, overwork, and burnout.

Paragraph 5

_____ 9. In recent years, several countries have prohibited digital nomads from working in their countries.

_____ 10. A number of countries have started issuing special digital nomad visas.

Paragraph 6

_____ 11. To make a living, digital nomads frequently do a number of different jobs simultaneously.

_____ 12. The number of digital nomads is decreasing.

Choose the best headings

Paragraph 1

1. Advice for becoming a digital nomad

2. How and where digital nomads work

Paragraph 2

1. The history of digital nomads

2. Digital nomads have scientific backgrounds

Paragraph 3

1. The disadvantages of being a digital nomad

2. Reasons why people want to become digital nomads

Paragraph 4

1. Solutions to common problems faced by digital nomads

2. Issues that face digital nomads who work overseas for several years

Paragraph 5

1. Countries that welcome digital nomads

2. The do's and don'ts of being a digital nomad

Paragraph 6

1. Things you need to do to become a digital nomad

2. Basic facts about digital nomads

Speaking

Talk about digital nomads.

A: I heard that your sister is living in Bali.

B: Yes, that's right. She is a digital nomad. She has been in Bali for a year. Before that, she was in Thailand and Vietnam.

A: What does she do exactly?

B: Mostly editing. She said that she has a lot of clients.

A: Doesn't she get lonely being away for so long?

B: No, I don't think so. We talk every week on zoom, and she is always chatting with our parents. She has so many friends all over the world. She seems really happy.

A: It sounds so exciting. I really envy her.

B: Why don't you give it a try? I noticed that you have a great website. Maybe you could use those skills to start a business designing websites.

Writing

Write about digital nomads.

Example:

Modern technology has made it easier to become a digital nomad. With a laptop computer and a smartphone, people have all the equipment they need for a nomadic life. If you have skills in IT, marketing, designing websites, or teaching, you can soon find work. As a digital nomad, you will have a lot of freedom, see new places, and be your own boss.

What are the advantages and disadvantages of being a digital nomad?
Check the internet and get information about the advantages and
disadvantages of being a digital nomad.

Example:

The number of digital nomads is increasing because the lifestyle is attractive.
However, there are both advantages and disadvantages. Here are some
examples. The best thing about being a digital nomad is that you get a lot of
freedom. You can choose where you work, and how many days you work.
You can take a vacation whenever you want. However, digital nomads face
some problems. It is easy to feel isolated and lonely. There are often language
problems.

Unit 5

E-waste

E-waste is short for electronic waste. It includes devices or components that are damaged or no longer used because the technology is out of date. E-waste comes from things such as televisions, computers, mobile phones, refrigerators, and microwave ovens. While there has been a lot of emphasis on recycling paper, metals, and other materials, e-waste has been ignored 5 and the seriousness of the problem is underestimated. E-waste is a massive environmental issue that is getting worse. It is essential that companies and individuals consider ways of addressing it. If e-waste is not disposed of properly, it will have negative impacts on the environment and humans. Let's look at some of the ways in which e-waste is disposed of. 10

E-waste is frequently sorted by hand. Then, it is washed, shredded, and reduced to small particles or powder. This is known as mechanical recycling. This process results in dust particles, which are released into the air causing pollution that can be harmful to animals and humans.

In some cases, e-waste is buried. Huge holes are dug in the land, and 15 e-waste is filled into the holes and covered with earth. Over a period of years, toxins from e-waste such as mercury and lead leak into the earth. Eventually, these toxins come into contact with water and end up in streams, rivers, lakes, and oceans. This contamination has a negative effect on animals, plants, and people. 20

Some e-waste is dumped illegally on empty land. Toxic materials in the waste contaminate the land, and have a negative effect on trees and plants in that area. Crops that are grown in those areas absorb the toxins and can make people sick. In some cases, dumped e-waste is taken to pieces by local people, who try to sell any valuable materials. Working conditions are bad and people become sick.

The above methods of disposal have negative effects on the environment. Governments and companies are seriously considering the best ways of managing e-waste, and better methods of recycling and reusing e-waste are being developed. One powerful weapon in the fight against e-waste is for individuals to change their behavior. Let's look at ways of minimizing the amount of e-waste that we generate.

Don't buy a new device. Try to repair the one you have

Some people constantly upgrade their devices when new technology comes out. This means they buy a new mobile phone almost every year. If you are worried about e-waste, you should postpone an upgrade, and carefully consider if your existing device can still be used. You will be surprised how often you can keep using what you have. Don't forget that most manufacturers offer a repair service. Repairing your device can extend the lifetime by several years.

Instead of putting an old device in the garbage, you should look for a way to reuse it

What happens if you have just bought a new mobile phone? What should you do with the old one? If it is still working, you should think of how you can keep using it. You can use it only for music or use it as a GPS device in your car. Another option is to donate an old device to an organization that will pass it on to someone who needs a device.

Try to return old or broken devices to manufacturers

It is becoming common for manufacturers to take back unwanted devices and either reuse some of the parts or recycle them. You might need to pay a small fee for this service, but it is better than leaving an old device in a drawer or putting it in the trash.

If you cannot repair or reuse a device, dispose of it at a special e-waste recycling center

If you have trouble repairing or reusing a device, you may have no choice but to dispose of it. In this case, you should do it responsibly, and find a reliable company that will recycle it. Make sure you take unwanted electronic items to a recycling center that specializes in e-waste.

Match the words

Match the words 1 – 15 with the answers a – o.

_____ 1. device
_____ 2. component
_____ 3. ignore
_____ 4. underestimate
_____ 5. dispose of
_____ 6. particles
_____ 7. huge
_____ 8. toxins
_____ 9. mercury
_____ 10. lead
_____ 11. contamination
_____ 12. dump
_____ 13. absorb
_____ 14. minimizing
_____ 15. generate

a. think something is less important than it really is
b. polluting or poisoning something
c. throw away, get rid of,
d. to take in or soak up something such as a liquid
e. very small pieces of matter
f. a heavy, silvery-white liquid metal
g. reduce something that is not desirable
h. produce, create, make
i. to dispose of rubbish in a careless way
j. a piece of equipment or part of a larger machine
k. massive, gigantic
l. a chemical element with the symbol Pb
m. refuse to take notice, disregard intentionally
n. harmful substances
o. a piece of electronic equipment that can connect to the internet, such as a smartphone, tablet or laptop computer

Answer the questions

Read questions 1 – 12 and choose the best answer from a – l.

Paragraph 1
_____ 1. What do we know about recycling e-waste?
_____ 2. What do we know about the effect of e-waste on the environment?

Paragraph 2
_____ 3. How is e-waste often sorted?
_____ 4. What is the problem with mechanical recycling?

Paragraph 3
_____ 5. Which toxins leak into the earth?
_____ 6. Where do toxins end up?

Paragraph 4

____ 7. Where is some e-waste dumped?

____ 8. Why do some local people become sick?

Paragraph 5

____ 9. What is the problem with the methods of disposal mentioned above?

____ 10. What can individuals do in the fight against e-waste?

Paragraph 6

____ 11. If you want to upgrade your phone, but are worried about e-waste, what should you do?

____ 12. If you return an old or broken device to a manufacturer, what do you need to do?

a. Change their behavior

b. It has been ignored and the seriousness of the problem underestimated

c. It is getting worse

d. They have negative effects on the environment

e. It results in dust particles, which cause air pollution

f. Pay a small fee

g. Manually

h. Working conditions are bad

i. In streams, rivers, lakes, and oceans

j. Postpone an upgrade

k. On empty land

l. Mercury and lead

Check the facts

Are these statements true (T), false (F), or not given (NG) according to the information in the passage?

Paragraph 1

_____ 1. The problem of e-waste has received a lot of attention.

_____ 2. E-waste is an extremely serious issue.

Paragraph 2

_____ 3. Mechanical recycling of e-waste has 6 main stages.

_____ 4. Dust created by mechanical recycling is collected automatically by new technology.

Paragraph 3

_____ 5. If you bury e-waste, you can be fined up to 1,000 USD by the government.

_____ 6. Toxins from e-waste that are buried immediately leak into the earth.

Paragraph 4

_____ 7. Toxic materials from dumped e-waste have a bad effect on trees and plants.

_____ 8. Local people are trying to prevent e-waste from being dumped illegally.

Paragraph 5

_____ 9. Governments are thinking about improving ways of managing e-waste.

_____ 10. Many consumers have no intention of changing their behavior.

Paragraph 6

_____ 11. You can use an old device for music or as a GPS.

_____ 12. If you pay some money, manufacturers will take back unwanted devices.

Choose the best headings

Paragraph 1

1. The issue of how to dispose of e-waste has attracted little attention

2. It is necessary to renew efforts to create e-waste

Paragraph 2

1. The need for improving air quality

2. Problems associated with mechanical recycling

Paragraph 3

1. Burying e-waste in holes results in contamination that affects animals, plants, and people

2. Putting e-waste into holes and burying it is a long-term solution

Paragraph 4

1. When e-waste is dumped illegally on empty land, toxins are collected and disposed of

2. Dumping e-waste on empty land has several negative effects

Paragraph 5

1. Governments want to improve ways of managing e-waste

2. Generation of e-waste cannot be minimized

Paragraph 6

1. Guidelines for purchasing new electronic devices

2. What should you do with an old device?

Speaking

Talk about e-waste.

A: Did you upgrade your mobile phone again?

B: Yes, I really wanted to get the latest model.

A: Do you really need a new phone every year? If everyone did that, we would soon have mountains of e-waste around us.

B: I didn't really consider that. Actually, I have several old phones that I am not using. I have no idea what to do with them.

A: You could use them for storing photos or music. If they are not broken or damaged, you could still trade them in or sell them.

B: Yes, I will think about that.

A: Or you could donate them to a charity. I heard that there is a place near here that helps homeless people who need phones, but cannot afford to buy one.

B: I'll check that on the internet, and drop them off as soon as I can. Thanks for the information.

Writing

Write about e-waste.

Example:

Today almost everyone has a mobile phone, a laptop, and other devices. The lifetime of these products is getting shorter as companies bring out new and better models. This creates a lot of e-waste. It is difficult to recycle e-waste, and a lot of it is disposed of illegally.

How can we reduce e-waste?

Check the internet and get information about how we can reduce e-waste.

Example:

The amount of e-waste is increasing rapidly. Here are some ways to reduce the amount of e-waste that is generated. Try to extend the life of your device by keeping it clean and handling it with care. Make sure the battery is in good shape and remember that it can be replaced if necessary. Instead of buying a new device, try to refresh or repair the one you have. Before you purchase something new, ask yourself if you can repair the device you are currently using. If it is completely broken, take it to a recycling center that specializes in e-waste.

Lack of sleep can lead to serious health problems

It is well known that a good night's sleep is essential. The average person needs about 8 hours of good-quality sleep in order to be able to function normally. Of course, there is variation in the amount of sleep needed, and some people may need more or less sleep. About one percent of the population only needs 6 hours of sleep a night.   5

Sleep problems seem to be increasing. In the region of 30 percent of people suffer from lack of sleep or poor-quality sleep. What effect does lack of sleep have on us? If we have a couple of sleepless nights, we will be tired the next day, feel down, and have difficulty concentrating on our work. But there will be no significant long-term effects on our general health. Usually,   10 we will get over the problem, and our sleep patterns will return to normal.

But what happens if you continue to have trouble sleeping? The cumulative effects of lack of sleep can be very serious. You will have difficulty functioning, be unable to focus on anything, and might fall asleep at your desk. There is a possibility that you will be involved in some kind of   15 accident, such as a car accident. Let's look at some of the serious health issues caused by chronic lack of sleep.

Chronic lack of sleep can lead to serious medical problems. It can have a bad effect on your heart and lead to high blood pressure, heart disease, heart attack, and stroke. Lack of sleep is also associated with diabetes. It is thought   20 that lack of sleep interferes with the body's ability to control blood sugar levels, resulting in an increased risk of diabetes. Research has shown that people who suffer from chronic lack of sleep tend to overeat. Consequently, they have trouble maintaining a healthy body weight, and often become obese. Lack of sleep can have a bad effect on mental health. Conditions such 25 as anxiety and depression are frequently found in people who experience chronic lack of sleep. In general, lack of sleep leads to significant negative effects on the quality of life of the individual, as well as an increased risk of death.

If you are worried about deterioration in the quality of your sleep, you 30 should consider the following factors, which have been shown to interfere with having a good night's sleep. If you use computers, mobile phones, and other devices just before you go to bed, this could be an issue. The blue light emitted by such devices will disrupt your sleep. So, it is advisable to avoid using them for an hour or two before going to bed. Drinking alcohol at night 35 is another factor that will result in poor sleep quality. Caffeine is also thought to disrupt your sleep patterns. It remains in your system for several hours. It is not advisable to drink coffee or tea at night.

There are several things that you can do to improve your sleep quality. Try to have a sleep schedule. Decide on fixed times for going to bed and 40 waking up every day, and keep to this schedule. Make a bedtime routine that will help you to unwind at the end of the day. For example, take a warm shower or bath, and change into a comfortable pair of pajamas. Read a book, do some relaxation exercises or listen to some healing music. Make your bedroom more comfortable by buying a new pillow, bedding, and mattress. 45 Make sure that your room is at a comfortable temperature. Your room should be quiet and have curtains that block out the light. Here are some other things that will help you to get a better night's sleep. Make sure that you go outside in the day and expose yourself to sunlight. Also try to get some physical exercise. Taking a quick walk in the park or doing some light 50 stretching exercises will make a big difference to how you sleep.

Match the words

Match the words 1 – 14 with the answers a – n.

_____ 1. essential
_____ 2. function
_____ 3. variation
_____ 4. get over
_____ 5. cumulative
_____ 6. chronic
_____ 7. stroke
_____ 8. diabetes
_____ 9. obese
_____ 10. anxiety
_____ 11. depression
_____ 12. deterioration
_____ 13. disrupt
_____ 14. unwind

a. relax, take it easy
b. overcome, solve, recover from
c. interrupt, interfere with
d. necessary, indispensable
e. a disease involving excessive body fat
f. to be able to work/live as usual
g. becoming progressively worse
h. feeling of worry or uneasiness
i. fluctuation, change
j. a disease where your blood sugar is too high
k. of an illness that continues for a long time
l. increasing in quantity, progressive
m. a mental condition, feeling of sadness, guilt
n. a medical condition where there is not enough blood flow to the brain, or where bleeding takes place

Answer the questions

Read questions 1 – 12 and choose the best answer from a – l.

Paragraph 1

_____ 1. How much sleep does the average person need?

_____ 2. What percentage of people only need 6 hours of sleep a day?

Paragraph 2

_____ 3. What do we know about sleep problems?

_____ 4. How many people suffer from sleep problems?

Paragraph 3

_____ 5. What do we know about the cumulative effects of lack of sleep?

_____ 6. If you continue to have trouble sleeping, what kind of accident might you have?

Paragraph 4

_____ 7. What can chronic lack of sleep lead to?

_____ 8. Which disease is lack of sleep associated with?

Paragraph 5

_____ 9. If you use devices before you sleep, what will disrupt your sleep?

_____ 10. What drinks should you avoid before you sleep?

Paragraph 6

_____ 11. For a sleep schedule, what two things do you need to decide on?

_____ 12. Why is it important to go outside in the day?

a. Alcohol, tea, and coffee

b. To expose yourself to sunlight

c. Serious medical problems

d. Blue light emitted by devices

e. Around 30 percent

f. Times for going to bed and waking up

g. About 8 hours

h. They can be very serious

i. They appear to be going up

j. Diabetes

k. About one percent of people

l. A car accident

Check the facts

Are these statements true (T), false (F), or not given (NG) according to the information in the passage?

Paragraph 1

_____ 1. Not everyone needs 8 hours of sleep a night.

_____ 2. The best way to ensure a good night's sleep is to have a sleep schedule.

Paragraph 2

_____ 3. If you cannot sleep, you should consult a doctor.

_____ 4. If you cannot sleep properly for one or two days, it will not have a long-term effect on your general health.

Paragraph 3

_____ 5. If you continue to have trouble sleeping, you might have difficulty functioning and be unable to focus.

_____ 6. You can avoid accidents by taking medication.

Paragraph 4

_____ 7. People who suffer from chronic lack of sleep often have eating problems and become obese.

_____ 8. People who have sleep problems may also suffer from mental problems.

Paragraph 5

_____ 9. To improve the quality of your sleep, it is a good idea to avoid using electronic devices before you go to bed.

_____ 10. Drinking alcohol at night will help you to sleep.

Paragraph 6

_____ 11. Your bedtime routine should usually include meditation.

_____ 12. The temperature and light in your bedroom are both important and will affect the quality of your sleep.

Choose the best headings

Paragraph 1

1. The amount of sleep people need varies
2. Less than 8 hours of sleep leads to health issues

Paragraph 2

1. Sleep problems can be treated by medication
2. The effects of a couple of sleepless nights

Paragraph 3

1. The effects of long-term lack of sleep
2. Car accidents can be avoided if you have enough medication

Paragraph 4

1. Lack of sleep has no long-term effects on quality of life
2. Medical problems that are a result of chronic lack of sleep

Paragraph 5

1. Improve the quality of your sleep by avoiding these things
2. How to improve your mental health

Paragraph 6

1. Make sure you consult a doctor if your sleep problems continue
2. Making changes to your sleep routine and bedroom will improve your sleep

Speaking

Talk about lack of sleep.

A: You were asleep in the seminar yesterday. Why are you so sleepy recently? Are you okay?

B: Not really. I'm not getting enough sleep. And when I do sleep, it is not a really deep sleep. Sometimes, I can't fall asleep even though I am really tired. This has been going on for months

A: Sleep is important. Lack of sleep can lead to serious health issues.

B: I know, but I'm finding it difficult to do anything about it. My doctor recommended sleeping tablets, but I am worried about getting addicted to them.

A: There are lots of things you can do to improve the situation. First of all, stop using a mobile phone or computer before you go to bed. They emit blue light, which will disrupt your sleep.

B: Ok. I'll try to do that.

A: And make a sleep schedule. Go to bed and wake up at a fixed time every day. Don't stay up all night watching movies. If you can afford it, think about getting some new bedding.

B: Ok. Thanks for the advice.

Writing

Write about lack of sleep.

Example:

The number of people with sleep problems is increasing. Chronic lack of sleep can lead to problems such as high blood pressure, and heart disease. If you have sleep problems, it is important to see a doctor. At the same time, there are several things that you can do to improve your sleep quality. Try to unwind before going to bed by taking a warm shower, doing some relaxation exercises, or reading a book.

Research question

What advice would you give someone who wants to improve the quality of their sleep?

Check the internet and get information about how to improve the quality of your sleep.

Example:

Here are some tips for improving your sleep. Decide on a time to go to bed and a time to wake up. It is important to keep to this schedule. Make sure that your sleeping environment is comfortable. If necessary, buy new pillows and sheets. The quality of your sleep will improve if you can get some exercise every day. Finally, you should avoid overeating, caffeine, and alcohol before you go to bed.

Prevention is better than cure

The expression 'prevention is better than cure' means that it is better to stop a problem from happening than to try to correct it after it has started. Recently, the term preventive medicine is being widely used. Preventive medicine focuses on ways of avoiding health issues before they start, and is being promoted by governments and healthcare professionals as a way 5 of preventing poor health and reducing healthcare costs. Let's look at how prevention is being used in dentistry to help people maintain good oral health.

Here are some facts about oral health that are shocking. Nearly 40 percent of adults do not visit the dentist regularly, and almost 30 percent of adults 10 have tooth decay. Around 75 percent of adults have had a tooth taken out. For ethnic minority groups, people on low incomes, and those with low levels of education, the situation is much worse. People in these groups often have serious problems with their teeth that require immediate treatment. With preventive measures, most of the above dental problems could be avoided. 15

There are several things you can do that will help you to have healthy teeth, and a great smile. These are brushing, flossing, using fluoride toothpaste, eating a healthy diet, and having regular checkups. If you include these in your daily life, you will be able to prevent any serious dental problems. 20

Brushing: Brushing your teeth twice daily is the most effective way of preventing oral health problems. How you brush is important, and you should learn how to do it properly. Your dentist or dental hygienist will give you advice on correct ways of brushing. Don't forget to brush your tongue. This helps to remove bacteria from your mouth, and makes your breath smell 25 fresher. Toothbrushes are important and should be replaced every 3 to 4 months. Your dental hygienist can give you advice on the best kind of brush to buy.

Flossing: Your dentist will probably recommend that you floss every day. Flossing is important because it removes small pieces of food and plaque 30 from between your teeth. There is a right way and a wrong way to floss, and it is important to get instruction. At your next dental appointment, ask your dental hygienist to show you how to floss correctly. Recent research suggests that there is a link between gum disease and other serious diseases such as heart disease, diabetes, and obesity. If you want to avoid gum disease, make 35 sure you brush and floss regularly.

Fluoride toothpaste: Fluoride is a mineral found in teeth and bones. It strengthens the outside part of your teeth, which consists of enamel. It prevents tooth decay and stops the growth of harmful bacteria in your mouth. Fluoride can be found in toothpaste, mouthwash, and supplements. 40 Next time you purchase toothpaste, make sure that it contains fluoride. It might cost more, but it will help to improve your oral health.

Eat a balanced diet: Eating a balanced diet is crucial because it protects your teeth by providing nutrients that they need. You should try to reduce the amount of sugar you consume, because bacteria in the mouth and sugar 45 create plaque which causes tooth decay. Drink plenty of water throughout the day and avoid sweet drinks. Vitamins are important for oral health. Eating a balanced diet will help you to get all of the vitamins you need to maintain your teeth.

Regular checkups: It is important to check for any problems with your teeth 50 or gums. You should visit your dentist at least once a year for a checkup. You should also have your teeth cleaned by a dental hygienist. This will stop plaque from accumulating on your teeth. With a checkup and cleaning, it will be possible to stop any problems before they become serious.

Match the words

Match the words 1 – 11 with the answers a – k.

_____ 1. prevention
_____ 2. cure
_____ 3. preventive
_____ 4. oral health
_____ 5. ethnic minority group
_____ 6. measure
_____ 7. fluoride
_____ 8. dental hygienist
_____ 9. plaque
_____ 10. gum disease
_____ 11. accumulate

a. step, action
b. biofilm of microorganisms that grow on the teeth
c. a mineral in bones and teeth, also in water etc
d. gums become swollen, red, and bleed
e. to restore health, get rid of an illness
f. health of the mouth, teeth, and gums
g. build up
h. the action of stopping something happening
i. people who belong to an ethnic group that is a small part of a population
j. promoting preventive health care to improve a patient's well-being, and prevent disease or death
k. a member of staff in a dental clinic who works to improve patients' dental hygiene

Answer the questions

Read questions 1 – 14 and choose the best answer from a – n.

Paragraph 1

_____ 1. What does preventive medicine focus on?
_____ 2. Why are governments promoting preventive medicine?

Paragraph 2

_____ 3. How many people have had a tooth removed?
_____ 4. Which groups of people have had serious problems with their teeth?

Paragraph 3

_____ 5. How often should you brush your teeth?
_____ 6. How frequently should you change your toothbrush?

Paragraph 4

_____ 7. Why is flossing important?

_____ 8. Who should you ask to show you how to brush correctly?

Paragraph 5

_____ 9. What is fluoride?

_____ 10. Which dental products contain fluoride?

Paragraph 6

_____ 11. Why should you reduce the amount of sugar you eat?

_____ 12. What kinds of drinks should you avoid?

Paragraph 7

_____ 13. How often should you visit your dentist?

_____ 14. What is the advantage of having your teeth cleaned by a dental hygienist?

---

a. As a way of preventing poor health and reducing healthcare costs

b. Every 3 to 4 months

c. Twice daily

d. Because bacteria in the mouth and sugar create plaque that causes tooth decay

e. About 75 percent

f. Ethnic minorities, people on low incomes, those with low levels of education

g. It removes small pieces of food and plaque from between your teeth

h. Toothpaste, mouthwash, and supplements

i. Ways of avoiding health issues before they start

j. At least once a year

k. Sweet drinks

l. It will prevent plaque from building up on your teeth

m. Your dental hygienist

n. A mineral found in teeth and bones

Check the facts

Are these statements true (T), false (F), or not given (NG) according to the information in the passage?

Paragraph 1

_____ 1. The term preventive medicine is being widely used.

_____ 2. Governments are spending too much money on research into tooth decay.

Paragraph 2

_____ 3. Almost 40 percent of adults fail to see a dentist regularly.

_____ 4. People in ethnic minority groups have better oral health than other people.

Paragraph 3

_____ 5. You should remember to brush your tongue.

_____ 6. It is important to learn how to brush properly and purchase an electric toothbrush.

Paragraph 4

_____ 7. Small pieces of food and plaque can be removed from between your teeth by flossing.

_____ 8. In some countries, fluoride is added to tap water.

Paragraph 5

_____ 9. Fluoride does not improve your oral health.

_____ 10. It is important to use toothpaste that contains fluoride.

Paragraph 6

_____ 11. You should drink plenty of water, tea, and sweet drinks.

_____ 12. You can get all the vitamins you need by eating a balanced diet.

Paragraph 7

_____ 13. A yearly checkup by a dentist is advisable.

_____ 14. Dental hygienists will advise you on how to maintain your weight.

Choose the best headings

Paragraph 1

1. Preventive medicine helps avoid health problems
2. Governments are increasing the cost of healthcare

Paragraph 2

1. Data on oral health show a lot of people have dental problems
2. Preventive measures do not solve any dental problems

Paragraph 3

1. To avoid bad oral health, it is important to brush regularly
2. Dental hygienists require several visits a year

Paragraph 4

1. The importance of flossing
2. Heart disease, diabetes and obesity are increasing

Paragraph 5

1. Oral health does not depend on what you eat or drink
2. The benefits of fluoride

Paragraph 6

1. You can eat as much sugar as you like
2. What you eat and drink will affect your oral health

Paragraph 7

1. Only make a dental appointment if you have a problem
2. The importance of regular checkups

Speaking

🔊 Talk about preventive medicine.

A: What's the matter?

B: I have toothache, and my gums are bleeding.

A: Did you make an appointment to see a dentist?

B: Not, yet. Actually, I haven't been to a dental clinic for a long time.

A: You should visit a dentist at least once a year for a checkup. And you should have your teeth cleaned by a dental hygienist. It's called preventive dentistry.

B: I will make an appointment as soon as possible. What is preventive dentistry exactly?

A: It involves taking action to prevent problems from occurring. It means that you should brush and floss daily, use fluoride toothpaste, and have regular checkups. If you do those things, you should be able to avoid toothache, gum problems, and other more serious issues.

B: It sounds like a lot of sense.

A: It is. You'd better make an appointment as soon as you can.

Writing

🔊 Write about preventive medicine.

Example:

The aim of preventive medicine is to avoid disease and illness. Instead of treating a health problem after it has developed, preventive medicine promotes healthy lifestyles that stop people from getting ill in the first place. Preventive medicine is important because it reduces the number of people with bad health, and lowers costs for governments.

....

....

....

....

....

Research question

What are some of the best ways to prevent disease?

Check the internet and get information about some of the best ways to prevent disease.

Example:

A lot of serious diseases are preventable. Let's look at some ways of avoiding diseases.

Make sure you eat food that is healthy
Exercise for 30 minutes a day
Quit smoking and drinking alcohol
Have your blood pressure checked
Have your cholesterol level checked

How to improve indoor air quality

2-1 The average person spends only about 8 percent of their time outside on a weekday. This means that the majority of time is spent indoors. Although there has been a lot of research on the quality of the air we breathe when we are outside, most people are not concerned about indoor air quality. Poor indoor air quality can have a negative effect on our health. In some 5 developing countries, indoor air pollution is a major health hazard. The main source of this pollution is the burning of coal and wood for heating and cooking. Many deaths occur as a result of indoor air pollution. In developed countries, indoor air quality issues are second-hand smoke, and fumes from gas stoves and kerosene heaters, which in some cases produce small particles 10 that remain in the air. Mold is also an issue.

2-2 One way to improve air quality at home and in the office is to have indoor plants. These release oxygen and absorb carbon dioxide. They also release water vapor and regulate humidity. This improves indoor air quality, and also eliminates harmful toxins. In the 1980s, researchers at NASA 15 were looking for ways to improve air quality in spacecraft. They conducted research on the effects of indoor plants in improving indoor air quality. The main result was that indoor plants can remove as much as 80 percent of toxins in the air over a period of 24 hours.

2-3 Since the NASA study, there has been a lot of other research on the 20 effects of indoor plants on air quality. Results have proved that indoor plants have positive effects on people and can improve their concentration and productivity by about 15 percent. They can also reduce stress levels, and boost your mood and general health. People who suffer from loneliness say that they feel much happier and healthier when they have indoor plants. For these reasons, indoor plants can be beneficial in your home or work environment.

Researchers set up an experiment to measure the benefits of indoor plants. Participants were asked to complete two tasks. The first task involved transferring an indoor plant from a small pot to a large one, and giving the plant fertilizer and water. As this was being done, researchers measured participants' blood pressure and heart rate. Results showed that people had normal blood pressure and heart rate. In the second task, which was carried out a day later, researchers instructed the participants to open a file on a computer and input numbers and sentences. When participants started inputting data, their blood pressure and heart rate increased significantly. From this research, scientists concluded that plants can provide psychological and physical health benefits.

People are now more aware of the dangers caused by poor indoor air quality. The benefits of having indoor plants at home and in the workplace have been confirmed scientifically through experimental research. There are, of course, additional measures that can be taken to ensure that you are living in an indoor environment where the air does not pose a threat to your health. Here are some examples of how to improve air quality at home.

Make sure you get some fresh air in your house. Open the windows for between 5 to 10 minutes a day.

Extractor fans should be installed in the kitchen, bathroom, and toilet to remove steam, smells, smoke, pollutants, and humidity. This will reduce the risk of mold.

For heating and cooking, use electricity or gas. Never use wood or coal as these pollute the air. If you use gas or paraffin to cook or heat, make sure your appliances are well-maintained. You should have them checked by a professional once a year.

Keep your room clean by vacuuming every day, and use a damp cloth to wipe the floor and other surfaces. This will significantly reduce the amount of dust in the air.

Match the words

Match the words 1 – 11 with the answers a – k.

_____ 1. major   a. control
_____ 2. health hazard   b. take in
_____ 3. fumes   c. significant, serious, important, substantial
_____ 4. mold   d. do away with, eradicate, wipe out, get rid of
_____ 5. absorb   e. wet, moist
_____ 6. regulate   f. perform, carry out
_____ 7. eliminate   g. job
_____ 8. conduct   h. show the truth of something by evidence
_____ 9. prove   i. gas or vapor that is a danger to a person's health
_____ 10. task   j. a potential source of danger to a person's health
_____ 11. damp   k. fungus that grows indoors in wet areas with no ventilation

Answer the questions

Read questions 1 – 12 and choose the best answer from a – l.

Paragraph 1

_____ 1. How long do most people spend outside on a weekday?

_____ 2. What type of air has research focused on?

Paragraph 2

_____ 3. What is the best way to have better air quality at home and in the office?

_____ 4. What was the goal of research carried out by NASA in the 1980's?

Paragraph 3

_____ 5. By how much do indoor plants improve concentration and productivity?

_____ 6. What do indoor plants reduce?

Paragraph 4

_____ 7. While participants were doing the first task, what did researchers measure?

_____ 8. What happened when participants started inputting data?

Paragraph 5

_____ 9. What are people more conscious of?

_____ 10. How were the benefits of indoor plants confirmed?

Paragraph 6

_____ 11. How often should you have appliances checked?

_____ 12. What should you use to wipe the floor?

---

a. Stress levels

b. By about 15 percent

c. About 8 percent of their time

d. Once a year

e. To have indoor plants

f. To improve air quality in spacecraft

g. A damp cloth

h. Through experimental research

i. Air we breathe when we are outside

j. Participants' blood pressure and heart rate

k. The dangers caused by poor indoor air quality

l. Their blood pressure and heart rate increased significantly

Check the facts

Are these statements true (T), false (F), or not given (NG) according to the information in the passage?

Paragraph 1

____ 1. The majority of people are not worried about indoor air quality.

____ 2. The sources of indoor air pollution in developing and developed countries are the same.

Paragraph 2

____ 3. Indoor plants control humidity.

____ 4. Indoor plants that can eliminate toxins were developed by NASA.

Paragraph 3

____ 5. In addition to the NASA study, a large amount of research on the effects of indoor plants has been conducted.

____ 6. Indoor plants had no positive effects on lonely people.

Paragraph 4

____ 7. Researchers asked participants to take care of an indoor plant.

____ 8. The second task was carried out several days after the first one was completed.

Paragraph 5

____ 9. Awareness of the dangers of poor indoor air quality was measured in several places using a questionnaire.

____ 10. There are other ways of making sure that the air in your home is not dangerous.

Paragraph 6

____ 11. It is a good idea to put extractor fans in the kitchen, bathroom, and toilet.

____ 12. Installing dust filters will monitor and reduce the amount of dust in the air.

Choose the best headings

Paragraph 1

1. Research on the air we breathe outside is necessary
2. Indoor air pollution has a bad effect on health

Paragraph 2

1. Indoor air quality can be improved by plants
2. Toxins were unaffected by indoor plants

Paragraph 3

1. Studies focusing on indoor plants had no results
2. Research on indoor plants showed they have various positive effects on people

Paragraph 4

1. An experiment was conducted to measure the benefits of indoor plants
2. Researchers asked participants to plant several small trees

Paragraph 5

1. Science has proved the positive effects of indoor plants
2. Improving indoor air quality with other methods is difficult

Paragraph 6

1. People need to take less action to clean up indoor air quality
2. There are a number of simple ways of improving indoor air quality

Speaking

Talk about indoor plants.

A: What are you going to do on the weekend?

B: I'm going to the garden center to look at some plants.

A: I didn't know you are interested in plants.

B: Recently, I have become interested in indoor plants. Where I work, the company has indoor plants in the offices and meeting rooms. In the beginning, I didn't really notice them. After a while, I realized that they seemed to make quite a big difference.

A: In what way?

B: Plants release oxygen and absorb carbon dioxide. They also control humidity. The air seems a lot cleaner. They seem to have a positive effect on people. So, I have decided to buy some indoor plants for my apartment.

A: That sounds interesting. Do you mind if I come along?

B: Not at all.

Writing

Write about indoor plants.

Example:

If you are worried about air quality at home or in your office, you should think about buying some indoor plants. They release oxygen, absorb carbon dioxide, and also eliminate harmful toxins. Indoor plants have a positive effect on people, and can reduce stress levels as well as improve your mood.

Research question

What are the benefits of having indoor plants?

Check the internet and get information about the benefits of having indoor plants.

Example:

Indoor plants have become popular because they have several positive effects. They reduce stress levels and can make you feel more relaxed. Looking after indoor plants is therapeutic. People with anxiety and depression find that looking after indoor plants improves their well-being. In fact, some clinics are prescribing indoor plants for people with mental illnesses.

Alternative treatments for mild depression

When you are sick, you go to a clinic and see a doctor. The doctor will ask you some questions about the problem you have, and will examine you. You may need to have a blood test, an X-ray, or some other tests. In most cases, the doctor will prescribe some medicine. Data on the use of medicine show that about 15 percent of people take 5 or more drugs a day, and about 5 7 percent of people take 8 or more drugs a day. The more medicines a person takes, the higher the chance that one of them will have a harmful side effect. Research has found that 10 percent of drugs prescribed are not suitable for patients. Overprescribing medicines is a serious problem, and the search for alternative treatments is attracting a lot of attention. 10

Let's take a look at how mild depression is usually treated. Doctors will probably encounter a lot of patients suffering from mild depression, and will prescribe antidepressants. However, there is now a movement toward alternative treatments to help people suffering from mild depression. An alternative treatment is defined as a non-standard medical treatment that is 15 used instead of conventional medicine. Here are some examples of alternative treatments.

Talking therapy

Talking therapy involves talking to a trained professional about your thoughts, feelings, and behavior. The aim is to help you manage your 20 problems. There are many kinds of talking therapy, but all of them are with a trained therapist. Therapy sessions can be one-to-one, in groups, by phone, by email, or on a video link. Therapists will help you to find answers to your problems. Some people suffering from mild depression say that talking therapy is as or more effective than taking medicine. 25

Mindfulness

The aim of mindfulness is to learn to concentrate and shut out negative thoughts. Mindfulness involves paying more attention to your thoughts, feelings, and things around you. It is about noticing and appreciating everyday things such as birds singing, the warmth of the sun, and the feeling 30 of a cool breeze on a hot day. Doing this makes you appreciate things you have taken for granted. This kind of awareness makes it easier to deal with problems such as stress, anxiety, and depression.

Peer support and mentoring

In peer support and mentoring, people use their own experiences to help 35 others in the group. In this therapy, you are matched with partners or groups of people who have had similar problems or experiences as your own. In some cases, these may be people who have recovered from problems such as depression, and are in a position to give advice and talk about how they overcame problems. 40

Supporting your physical health and well-being

This therapy introduces ways of taking better care of your physical health and well-being. Programs focus on basic life skills. For example, simple ideas for cooking balanced and nutritious meals. In these group activities, a volunteer will lead a cooking class and show you what ingredients to buy 45 and how to put them into a recipe. Taking part in these kinds of activities will help you to get stronger, give you confidence, and make you feel happier.

Arts and creative therapy

This type of therapy includes drawing, painting, sewing, knitting, woodwork, writing, music, and other similar activities. In this therapy, you 50 use your hands to do things that will take your mind off problems, and make you feel positive, and more confident. The goal is to help you to talk about difficult issues you are facing, and how to overcome them.

Ecotherapy

Ecotherapy is also known as nature therapy and green therapy. It 55 involves getting outside in nature and taking part in activities such as conservation projects, growing vegetables, and gardening. Other options are to join people walking or cycling through forests and other areas of nature.

Match the words

Match the words 1 – 11 with the answers a – k.

_____ 1. alternative
_____ 2. mild
_____ 3. depression
_____ 4. prescribe
_____ 5. overprescribe
_____ 6. medication
_____ 7. encounter
_____ 8. conventional
_____ 9. anxiety
_____ 10. therapy
_____ 11. overcome

a. a feeling of worry, nervousness
b. prescribe too many drugs
c. normal, standard
d. get over, solve, handle a problem
e. a mental condition, feeling of sadness, guilt
f. one or more things available as a choice
g. not serious, not severe
h. meet
i. a doctor advises the use of a medicine in writing
j. a drug or other form of medicine to treat an illness
k. treatment of mental problems using psychology as a base

Answer the questions

Read questions 1 – 16 and choose the best answer from a – p.

Paragraph 1

_____ 1. What percentage of people take 5 or more drugs a day?
_____ 2. What percentage of drugs are not suitable for patients?

Paragraph 2

_____ 3. What kind of drugs will the majority of doctors prescribe for mild depression?
_____ 4. How is an alternative treatment defined?

Paragraph 3

_____ 5. What is the aim of talking therapy?
_____ 6. How many different methods of conducting talking therapy sessions are mentioned?

Paragraph 4

_____ 7. What is the aim of mindfulness?
_____ 8. In mindfulness, what do you need to focus on?

Paragraph 5

_____ 9. In peer support and mentoring, what do people use to help others in the group?

_____ 10. In peer support and mentoring, who are you matched with?

Paragraph 6

_____ 11. In supporting your physical and mental well-being, what do programs focus on?

_____ 12. What will these kinds of activities help you to do?

Paragraph 7

_____ 13. In arts and creative therapy, how many types of therapy are mentioned?

_____ 14. How will arts and creative therapy make you feel?

Paragraph 8

_____ 15. What is ecotherapy also known as?

_____ 16. Where do most activities take place?

---

a. To help you manage your problems
b. Your thoughts, feelings, and things around you
c. Antidepressants
d. Positive and more confident
e. About 15 percent
f. 5
g. To learn to concentrate and shut out negative thoughts
h. Outside in nature
i. Nature therapy and green therapy
j. As a non-standard medical treatment used instead of conventional medicine
k. 7
l. 10 percent
m. Their own experiences
n. Partners or groups of people who have had similar problems or experiences
o. Basic life skills
p. To get stronger, have more confidence, and feel happier

Check the facts

Are these statements true (T), false (F), or not given (NG) according to the information in the passage?

Paragraph 1

_____ 1. Evidence shows that in the region of 15 percent of people take 5 or more drugs a day.

_____ 2. Doctors tend to give patients too many drugs, but this is not a big issue.

Paragraph 2

_____ 3. Doctors rarely see patients suffering from mild depression.

_____ 4. Conventional medicine is considered to be more effective than alternative medicine.

Paragraph 3

_____ 5. In all kinds of talking therapy, a trained therapist is present.

_____ 6. Therapy sessions can sometimes last several days.

Paragraph 4

_____ 7. Mindfulness has been used in half of all cases of depression.

_____ 8. Mindfulness makes it easier to deal with stress, anxiety, and depression.

Paragraph 5

_____ 9. This program used specialist doctors who have recovered from depression.

_____ 10. In this program, you will be able to talk to nurses and doctors only.

Paragraph 6

_____ 11. Basic life skills are the main focus of this program.

_____ 12. This program involves a short test of the skills learned.

Paragraph 7

_____ 13. In arts and creative therapy, you generally use your hands.

_____ 14. Arts and creative therapy is the most effective of all types of alternative treatments.

Paragraph 8

_____ 15. Ecotherapy takes place outdoors.

_____ 16. There is a lot of evidence to suggest that ecotherapy is ineffective.

Choose the best headings

Paragraph 1

1. Issues prescribing medicine
2. The problem of side effects

Paragraph 2

1. Few patients have mild depression
2. There is a trend toward alternative treatments for mild depression

Paragraph 3

1. The goal of talking therapy is to help you cope with your issues
2. Trained therapists will give medicine to patients

Paragraph 4

1. Mindfulness teaches you to concentrate and pay attention to positive things
2. Controlling how you react to problems is important

Paragraph 5

1. Peer support and mentoring involves sharing experiences
2. Peer support and mentoring is always one to one

Paragraph 6

1. Physical health and well-being activities make people stronger, more confident, and happier
2. Learning about nutrition

Paragraph 7

1. In this therapy, you have to work in large groups
2. Using your hands has a number of positive benefits

Paragraph 8

1. Ecotherapy is important because you can be alone
2. Ecotherapy involves being active and getting outside

Speaking

Talk about alternative treatments.

A: Are you feeling any better recently?

B: Yes, I am feeling a lot better. I stopped taking the tablets the doctor prescribed. They made me feel worse.

A: Really? Is it okay to do that?

B: I think so. I did some research on alternative treatments. I joined a peer support and mentoring group. We meet once a week online. The group leader is a trained psychologist.

A: What kind of people are in the group?

B: Some people have problems with anxiety. Others have partially recovered from the problem. I find it really useful to talk to people who have the same problem as I do.

A: What actually happens in a meeting?

B: We talk about our problems, and give each other advice and support. The group leader also gives us advice, and motivates us to help ourselves. For me, it is much more effective than taking medication. If you want to know more about it, do a net search for alternative treatments for mild depression. There is a lot of information available.

Writing

Write about alternative treatments.

Example:

The majority of doctors treat mild depression by prescribing drugs. Recently, alternative treatments have received considerable attention. In some cases, they have proved to be more effective than medication. One such example is mindfulness, which helps people to control negative thoughts by noticing and appreciating everyday things.

Research question

What are some alternative treatments for mild depression?

Check the internet and get information about alternative treatments for mild depression.

Example:

There are many alternative treatments that can help relieve the symptoms of depression. Several herbs are successful in treating depression. These herbs improve your memory and other brain functions. Exercise has a positive effect on people who suffer from mild depression. Most forms of exercise are good, but walking, running, and swimming seem to be extremely effective in relieving symptoms.

Car-free zones

A car-free zone is part of a town or city that is for the use of pedestrians only. Motor vehicles may not enter these areas except to pick up or deliver goods. Car-free zones are also known as auto-free zones and pedestrian zones. In the UK, they are called pedestrian precincts, and in the US and Australia, they are known as pedestrian malls or pedestrian streets. 5

The concept of vehicle-free zones has a long history. From about the year 1800, it was common for cities in Europe to have shopping arcades. These were narrow streets with shops on either side, floors decorated with colored tiles, and roofs made of glass that gave the street a light, airy atmosphere. Shoppers could enjoy walking through the arcade without encountering any 10 vehicles. In London, several of these arcades, that were built in 1818, have survived and are popular with visitors to the city today. Similar arcades were opened in Paris in 1784. From the 1920's, some busy shopping streets in major cities in countries such as France and Germany started to become pedestrianized. 15

As people became more affluent and could afford to buy a car, it became common to drive into the city center on weekends to go shopping or eat at a restaurant. However, this trend caused a lot of problems. Cities found that they needed more parking spaces for cars. Valuable land in the center of the city was used to build car parks, and there was less land available 20 for building houses and apartments. City centers became increasingly crowded, and air quality deteriorated as a result of exhaust gas emitted by cars. Noise pollution was another issue. Cars and traffic jams give off heat. This increases the temperature in urban areas, and has a negative effect on the environment. Because people were able to drive into city centers, fewer 25 people used public transport such as buses, trains, and trams. Additionally, almost nobody walked or cycled into the city center.

In towns and cities that suffered from traffic congestion, local governments and citizens became increasingly concerned about the problems caused by cars. Many citizens' groups called for steps to be taken to reduce 30 traffic in city centers. Such initiatives did not get very far, and were opposed by businesses, shops, and restaurants that were against car-free zones. Owners of these businesses feared that there would be fewer customers, and that sales and profits would go down. Towns and cities decided to take small steps to help people get accustomed to car-free zones. Some cities decided 35 to have one car-free Sunday a month. Others banned older cars that caused more air pollution. Larger cities introduced charges, and drivers needed to pay to take their car into the city center. In this way, the number of cars entering city centers was reduced.

After new car-free zones were introduced, a lot of people were surprised 40 to find that they had a positive effect on the economy and the environment. For shops in car-free zones, sales went up by about 30 percent. Noise pollution went down by 10 decibels on car-free days. Levels of nitrogen dioxide fell by 40 percent in some cities. More people walked or cycled into the city center, and others took public transport. This meant that people 45 could include exercise in their daily life, and in this way their general health improved. As people took public transport more frequently, train and bus companies decided to invest an increasing amount of money in services. When the quality of public transport went up, more people left their cars at home and took the train or bus into the city center. 50

It is probable that increasing numbers of towns and cities will set up car-free zones or extend ones that are already in operation. However, this kind of plan is difficult to put into practice, and takes both time and effort. Cooperation among groups such as town planners, environmentalists, public health professionals, businesses, and citizens is required. The creation of 55 more car-free zones will result in happier and healthier residents, as well as more profitable shops and restaurants. It will also improve air quality in city centers and help to reduce global warming.

Match the words

Match the words 1 – 9 with the answers a – i.

_____ 1. pedestrians
_____ 2. pedestrianized
_____ 3. deteriorated
_____ 4. exhaust gas
_____ 5. emit
_____ 6. congestion
_____ 7. initiatives
_____ 8. banned
_____ 9. in operation

a. being used
b. prohibited, not allowed
c. traffic jams, large number of vehicles not moving
d. get progressively worse over a period of time
e. people who travel on foot on a road or sidewalk
f. fumes emitted by car and truck engines
g. to produce and discharge gas or fumes
h. actions
i. shut a street or area to traffic so it is used by pedestrians only

Answer the questions

Read questions 1 – 12 and choose the best answer from a – l.

Paragraph 1

_____ 1. Who are the main users of car-free zones?

_____ 2. What are car-free zones called in the UK?

Paragraph 2

_____ 3. When were shopping arcades first built in Europe?

_____ 4. In which city do arcades built in 1818 remain?

Paragraph 3

_____ 5. As more people drove into city centers on weekends, what did cities need?

_____ 6. Why did air quality get worse?

Paragraph 4

_____ 7. Why were businesses against car-free zones?

_____ 8. Why did cities ban older cars?

Paragraph 5

_____ 9. By how much did sales go up in shops in car-free zones?

_____ 10. By how much did nitrogen dioxide levels fall?

Paragraph 6

_____ 11. Why is it difficult to set up or extend car-free zones?

_____ 12. How many groups should be involved in cooperation?

a. From about the year 1800

b. As a result of exhaust gas emitted by cars

c. More parking spaces

d. Because they caused more air pollution

e. By 40 percent

f. Because it is difficult to put into practice, and takes time and effort

g. 5

h. Pedestrian precincts

i. By about 30 percent

j. London

k. Pedestrians

l. They thought there would be fewer customers, and that sales and profits would go down

Check the facts

Are these statements true (T), false (F), or not given (NG) according to the information in the passage?

Paragraph 1

_____ 1. Delivery vehicles are allowed to enter car-free zones.

_____ 2. Another expression for car-free zones is pedestrian zones.

Paragraph 2

_____ 3. Vehicle-free zones are a concept that started quite recently.

_____ 4. From the 1920's, vehicles were banned from all shopping streets in cities in France and Germany.

Paragraph 3

_____ 5. With more vehicles entering the city centers on weekends, there were issues with air quality and noise pollution.

_____ 6. Public transport had fewer users and closed down in many cases.

Paragraph 4

_____ 7. Requests made by citizens' groups were opposed by businesses, shops, and restaurants.

_____ 8. Drivers of old cars were unable to drive into the city center.

Paragraph 5

_____ 9. As a result of introducing new car-free zones, more people walked or cycled into the city.

_____ 10. With increasing use of public transport, train and bus companies reduced investment.

Paragraph 6

_____ 11. The number of car-free zones will probably go up.

_____ 12. Environmentalists and public health professionals were excluded from discussions.

Choose the best headings

Paragraph 1

1. Origins of car-free zones
2. Naming of car-free zones in various countries

Paragraph 2

1. How car-free zones started and spread
2. Car-free zones became unpopular

Paragraph 3

1. Problems caused by driving into cities on weekends
2. Solutions for issues caused by car-free zones

Paragraph 4

1. Businesses and citizens had the same plans
2. Citizens' groups and owners of shops and businesses had different opinions about car-free zones

Paragraph 5

1. Although new car-free zones were introduced the results were negative
2. Many positive results came out of the introduction of car-free zones

Paragraph 6

1. Many people are opposed to car-free zones
2. The future of car-free zones

Speaking

Talk about car-free zones.

A: What is the best thing about the city you live in?

B: It has a lot of good points, but I really like the car-free zones. Most of the central area has no cars at all.

A: That sounds nice. But how do people access the area?

B: We have trams, buses, and a subway. Access is easy, reliable, and cheap. Most central business districts are empty on weekends. But ours is a magnet for locals, people from out of town, and tourists. There are so many shops, restaurants, and events. If you get bored with shopping or eating, you can enjoy walking around and looking at the events and exhibitions.

A: I guess it must be good for the economy.

B: Yes, shops are all making a lot of money, and restaurants and cafes are packed most of the time.

Writing

Write about car-free zones.

Example:

More and more cities are making car-free zones. There are so many advantages. Air quality improves and noise pollution is reduced. More residents cycle or walk into the city center, and their health and well-being improve. Shops and restaurants have more customers, and make more profits.

What are the main advantages of car-free zones?

Check the internet and get information about the main advantages of car-free zones.

Example:

Car-free zones were recently created in the cities of Oslo and Hamburg. The main advantages of this change are as follows:

A reduction in greenhouse gases, air pollution, noise, and temperature.
An increase in green spaces, and more opportunity to meet and talk to people.
An increase in people walking and cycling.
A general improvement in public health.

Lifestyle diseases

Lifestyle diseases are the result of daily habits that have a negative effect on health. They include, lack of exercise, bad diet, alcohol, drugs, and smoking tobacco. These habits are associated with heart disease, obesity, diabetes, cancer, and other diseases. Lifestyle diseases are responsible for 71 percent of all deaths annually, and the number of people with lifestyle diseases is increasing. These diseases are expensive to treat, and are putting pressure on health services. Consequently, governments are looking for ways of encouraging people to change their lifestyles.

The main question for governments is how to encourage people to lead a healthier lifestyle. Taxes are important in reducing lifestyle diseases. Governments have been taxing alcohol and tobacco for many years. Studies have found that a 10 percent increase in the price of cigarettes results in a 5 percent decrease in sales of tobacco. When alcohol prices are increased, there is a similar reduction in consumption. Governments also use public information campaigns to discourage habits such as smoking tobacco and drinking alcohol. In many countries, cigarette packets carry health warnings such as 'smoking kills'. Alcoholic drinks also have health warnings such as 'alcohol causes cancer'.

The above methods of promoting healthy lifestyles have been relatively successful, but in recent years, new ideas have been introduced. There has been more emphasis on programs with financial incentives. For example, if people join a scheme to improve their lifestyle by taking exercise, quitting smoking, and having a healthier diet, they will get cash rewards or vouchers from the government that can be exchanged for goods. Preliminary studies have shown that such incentive schemes work better if they are delivered using the latest mobile technology. Activity data can be collected by smartphone motion sensors. Participants can set goals, and get immediate access to find out how much progress they have made. Participants can share their progress with family and friends, which tends to increase motivation. In this way, the effectiveness of a program can be increased.

New methods of encouraging people to give up bad habits and adopt good ones have been put forward. Incentive schemes aimed at improving lifestyles by getting people to do more exercise have been set up in several countries. A scheme in Singapore that rewards people for taking exercise has been extremely successful. It is called 'the national step challenge' and nearly 30 percent of the population enrolled in it. Citizens received rewards if they did a certain amount of exercise, such as jogging or walking. Participants wore wearable devices, which recorded how many steps they had taken. Individuals earned health points, which could be exchanged for rewards of up to 10 US dollars.

Another incentive scheme has been established in the UK, where participants receive cash rewards for adopting healthy habits. The government has allocated 70 million pounds to the national health service to run a program that will target overweight or obese people. These people will be encouraged to take part in weight management programs. Some people will be provided with access to a personal trainer, who will help them to lose weight through exercise and healthy eating programs. At the same time, similar incentive schemes are being developed. In Scotland, a special program called 'give up for baby' has focused on encouraging pregnant mothers who smoke to quit the habit. Similar schemes have been set up that are aimed at helping people who have diabetes.

Lifestyle diseases are a serious concern for governments, particularly because of the cost of treatment. The standard methods of getting people to adopt healthier lives have had some success. New methods such as using financial incentives to get people to change their lifestyles are important, and have a lot of potential. From the results of the schemes in Singapore and the UK, it can be seen that incentives in the form of small cash payments are more effective in encouraging people to change their behavior than standard methods. As more of these schemes are introduced around the world, it is likely that the number of people with lifestyle diseases will be reduced.

Match the words

Match the words 1 – 11 with the answers a – k.

_____ 1. obesity
_____ 2. encourage
_____ 3. promote
_____ 4. financial incentives
_____ 5. participants
_____ 6. adopt
_____ 7. enroll
_____ 8. wearable
_____ 9. allocate
_____ 10. concern
_____ 11. standard

a. people who take part in a program
b. reward with money or other benefits
c. register as a member of a program
d. something that can be worn
e. normal, conventional
f. distribute
g. something that causes worry
h. take, take up, follow or use
i. advertise or support a program
j. help a person to feel confident to achieve a goal
k. a medical condition where there is too much body fat

Answer the questions

Read questions 1 – 12 and choose the best answer from a – l.

Paragraph 1

_____ 1. What do we know about the number of people with lifestyle diseases?

_____ 2. What are governments looking for?

Paragraph 2

_____ 3. For how long has there been a tax on alcohol and tobacco?

_____ 4. How do governments discourage smoking and drinking?

Paragraph 3

_____ 5. What do people get if they join a scheme to improve their lifestyle?

_____ 6. How is activity data collected?

Paragraph 4

_____ 7. How many Singaporeans took part in 'the national step challenge'?

_____ 8. How were steps recorded?

Paragraph 5

_____ 9. What kind of programs are obese people encouraged to take part in?

_____ 10. Who did the program 'give up for baby' target?

Paragraph 6

_____ 11. Why are governments concerned about lifestyle diseases?

_____ 12. Which is the best method of getting people to adopt healthy lifestyles, taxing tobacco and alcohol, or financial incentives?

a. For many years

b. By smartphone motion sensors

c. By wearable devices

d. Weight management programs

e. By public information campaigns

f. Because of the cost of treatment

g. Financial incentives

h. It is increasing

i. Cash rewards or vouchers

j. Pregnant mothers who smoke

k. Almost 30 percent of the population

l. Methods of encouraging people to change their lifestyles

Check the facts

Are these statements true (T), false (F), or not given (NG) according to the information in the passage?

Paragraph 1

_____ 1. Five examples are given of daily habits that have a negative effect on health.

_____ 2. Health services are refusing to treat patients with lifestyle diseases.

Paragraph 2

_____ 3. Taxes on tobacco and alcohol were stopped over a decade ago.

_____ 4. Alcoholic drinks carry health warnings such as 'smoking kills'.

Paragraph 3

_____ 5. The latest way of encouraging people to improve their lifestyle involves financial incentives.

_____ 6. Sharing progress with friends and family involved a drop in effectiveness of the program.

Paragraph 4

_____ 7. Currently, the only country using an incentive scheme is Singapore.

_____ 8. People who joined gyms or sports clubs received free advice.

Paragraph 5

_____ 9. In some cases, participants in the UK program get advice from a personal trainer.

_____ 10. People with diabetes were considered to be unsuitable for this scheme.

Paragraph 6

_____ 11. The main reason governments are worried about lifestyle diseases is the cost of treatment.

_____ 12. As a result of more new schemes worldwide, the number of people with lifestyle diseases will probably go down.

Choose the best headings

Paragraph 1

1. To prevent lifestyle diseases, governments want people to pay more tax
2. Diseases such as heart disease and obesity are linked to daily habits that have a negative effect on health

Paragraph 2

1. How to motivate people to have healthier habits
2. Public information campaigns are not successful in getting people to change their lifestyle

Paragraph 3

1. Governments have failed to introduce any successful programs aimed at changing lifestyles
2. A new scheme where people receive money or vouchers has recently been introduced

Paragraph 4

1. A large number of people have been unable to switch from bad habits to healthy habits
2. A number of countries have set up schemes where participants can get money or vouchers

Paragraph 5

1. A number of incentive schemes have been set up in the UK
2. The UK has had little success with incentive schemes

Paragraph 6

1. Standard methods of making people change their lifestyles have been extremely successful
2. People who receive financial incentives are able to make changes to their lifestyle

Speaking

Talk about promoting healthy lifestyles.

A: You have lost a lot of weight. Did you go on a diet?

B: I joined a government exercise scheme called 'step it out'. It has really helped me.

A: What does that involve?

B: You have to do 30 minutes of light exercise a day. I have been doing it for 3 months. I use my smartphone to record how many steps I have taken.

A: How do you motivate yourself?

B: There are some financial incentives. If you reach your goals every week, you get some points or vouchers. You can spend them in supermarkets.

A: The incentive system sounds like a good program.

B: I am enjoying it a lot, and the vouchers motivate me to keep exercising. I have found that exercising is fun. In fact, I will probably continue even after the program is over.

Writing

Write about lifestyle diseases.

Example:

Lifestyle diseases are caused by unhealthy choices in daily life. To avoid lifestyle diseases, you should do the following. Avoid eating junk food. Eat vegetables, and fresh fruit. Do some kind of physical exercise such as walking for 30 minutes a day. Reduce your weight by eating low-calorie, fat-free food. Also, cut down on the amount of sugar, salt, and oil you eat.

Research question

What methods do governments use to make people improve their lifestyles?
Check the internet and get information about methods governments use to make people improve their lifestyles.

Example:

Governments have used various methods to make people improve their lifestyles. Taxes on alcohol and cigarettes are one example. Public health campaigns with health warnings on cigarette packs and bottles of alcohol have also been used. Now, governments around the world are offering cash incentives and vouchers to encourage people to improve their lifestyles. This type of program seems to have a lot of potential.

Heatwaves

A heatwave is a long period of very hot weather. It is classified as a case of extreme weather, and as a natural disaster. Heatwaves are thought to be due to global warming and are becoming more frequent, widespread, and severe. It is feared that if climate change continues at the present rate, heatwaves will last longer, and have higher temperatures. Heatwaves kill far ₅ more people in the United States than other natural disasters. Typically, 1,500 Americans living in cities die every year as a result of extreme heat. Deaths from tornadoes, earthquakes, and floods combined are less than 200.

People find it difficult to think of heatwaves as natural disasters because they do not cause a lot of highly visible damage. With tornadoes, you can see ₁₀ trees, houses, bridges, and utility poles that have been severely damaged. You can also see cars and trucks that have been overturned. But with heatwaves, there is little evidence of damage except for the surfaces of roads, which sometimes melt, and farm animals that die. For this reason, people are not aware of the dangers of heatwaves. ₁₅

Many victims of heatwaves are old, have little money, and live in areas that have high levels of crime and poverty. They have little or no access to transportation, and often live in homes with no air-conditioning. A large number of victims are men living alone in one room. Cities have tried to reduce the effect of heatwaves by establishing special emergency teams that ₂₀ respond quickly to heatwaves. They issue heatwave warnings, and set up special emergency centers, where residents can get help. Emergency teams visit vulnerable people to check up on their well-being.

Governments and policy makers want to make people more aware of the dangers of heatwaves. To do this, they have decided to name heatwaves, measure them, and also rank them in terms of severity. Tropical storms have had human names since the 1950s. This makes it easier to issue warnings to the public and to increase media coverage of the event. Governments hope that naming heatwaves will make people take more notice of their potential impact and associated dangers. Throughout the world, extreme heat kills 5 million people a year, and countries are trying to raise people's awareness. Athens, which is the hottest capital city in Europe, has a 'chief heat officer'. Greece is the first country in Europe to have such a role.

In Australia, extreme heat kills more people than other natural disasters. People over the age of 75 who have medical conditions such as heart disease, and those with disabilities, are particularly vulnerable to extreme heat. It is easy for these groups of people to become dehydrated and get heatstroke, the medical term for which is hyperthermia. Heatstroke is classified as a medical emergency, and can result in death. Unfortunately, most people who are at risk, such as old people and the very young, do not take any precautions or try to stay safe. Less than half of people over 65 follow heat emergency recommendations such as drinking a lot of water.

With heatwaves increasing in frequency, duration, and severity, it is necessary to plan ahead and think about how you, your family, friends, and neighbors can stay safe when the next heatwave hits. Here are some suggestions that will help you to minimize risk when temperatures rise dramatically.

Avoid going outside when temperatures are high.

If you have to go out, make sure you take some water with you.

Even if you do not feel thirsty, it is important to drink a lot of water.

Use fans and air-conditioning, and keep blinds and curtains shut.

Taking a shower with cool water can help to lower your body temperature.

If you feel sick, call the local nurse or a doctor.

Match the words

Match the words 1 – 16 with the answers a – p.

_____ 1. heatwave

_____ 2. extreme weather

_____ 3. a natural disaster

_____ 4. visible

_____ 5. overturned

_____ 6. establish

_____ 7. respond

_____ 8. vulnerable

_____ 9. severity

_____ 10. media coverage

_____ 11. raise

_____ 12. awareness

_____ 13. dehydrated

_____ 14. heatstroke

_____ 15. precaution

_____ 16. minimize

a. major adverse event, flood, hurricane etc.

b. can be seen easily

c. react, reply

d. at risk, susceptible/exposed to danger

e. reporting of news on TV and in newspapers

f. degree of something bad such as weather/pain

g. increase, lift, elevate, bring up

h. weather event that is very different from usual

i. bring into existence

j. turned over, upside down

k. a period of excessively hot weather

l. having lost a large amount of water from the body

m. a condition caused by the body overheating

n. action taken in advance to prevent something bad

o. reduce something bad to the smallest amount

p. knowledge or perception of a situation or fact

Answer the questions

Read questions 1 – 12 and choose the best answer from a – l.

Paragraph 1

_____ 1. How are heatwaves classified?

_____ 2. How many people die in the US every year as a result of extreme heat?

Paragraph 2

_____ 3. Why don't people consider heatwaves as a natural disaster?

_____ 4. What visible damage of heatwaves can be seen?

Paragraph 3

_____ 5. Who are typical victims of heatwaves?

_____ 6. Who do emergency teams visit?

Paragraph 4

_____ 7. How many people die worldwide as a result of extreme heat?

_____ 8. Which was the first country to appoint a chief heat officer?

Paragraph 5

_____ 9. Which groups of people are vulnerable to extreme heat?

_____ 10. What is the medical term for heatstroke?

Paragraph 6

_____ 11. What should you do if you need to go out?

_____ 12. What should you do if you feel unwell?

a. Because they do not cause a lot of visible damage

b. Road surfaces melt and farm animals die

c. Call the local nurse or a doctor

d. 5 million a year

e. People who are at risk, vulnerable people

f. Greece

g. As a case of extreme weather and a natural disaster

h. People over 75 with medical conditions and those with disabilities

i. Take some water with you

j. Old men who live alone

k. 1,500

l. Hyperthermia

Check the facts

Are these statements true (T), false (F), or not given (NG) according to the information in the passage?

Paragraph 1

_____ 1. Heatwaves are declining in number and are less serious than previously.

_____ 2. Earthquakes are responsible for more deaths than heatwaves.

Paragraph 2

_____ 3. Damage caused by tornadoes is extremely visible.

_____ 4. People are not aware of the dangers of heatwaves because there is almost no information in the media.

Paragraph 3

_____ 5. In order to reduce the effects of heatwaves, some cities set up special emergency teams.

_____ 6. Special emergency centers treated 20,000 people with heatstroke.

Paragraph 4

_____ 7. Heatwaves have been given human names for a long time.

_____ 8. Many countries around the world consider it is essential to increase people's knowledge of the dangers of heatwaves.

Paragraph 5

_____ 9. People who are particularly vulnerable to extreme heat are over the age of 75 with medical problems.

_____ 10. At present, there are no emergency recommendations for heatwaves.

Paragraph 6

_____ 11. Heatwaves last longer than they used to.

_____ 12. Local nurses will visit the homes of vulnerable people in heatwaves.

Choose the best headings

Paragraph 1

1. How to prevent heatwaves
2. What are heatwaves?

Paragraph 2

1. Tornadoes cause more damage because they increase in intensity
2. Because heatwaves cause little visible damage, people are not aware of how dangerous they are

Paragraph 3

1. People who are most seriously affected by heatwaves live in downtown areas
2. Cities are taking action to mitigate the effects of heatwaves

Paragraph 4

1. Increasing awareness of the threat caused by heatwaves is the goal of governments and policy makers
2. All European cities have hired specialists on heatwaves

Paragraph 5

1. Groups of people that are vulnerable to heatwaves in Australia
2. At risk people learn to survive by following heatwave recommendations

Paragraph 6

1. Governments are continuing to establish guidelines
2. Risk can be reduced by following simple suggestions

Speaking

2·46 Talk about heatwaves.

A: I just checked the weather forecast for the next two weeks on my computer. Look at this.

B: It's going to be over 35 degrees every day. That's way above the average temperature for the time of year.

A: It's a heatwave. It's going to be like the one we had three years ago.

B: Is there anything we should be doing to prepare for this?

A: Let's start by getting the fans out of the storeroom. Then, let's make sure that the air-conditioners are working properly.

B: I think that we should call your parents to check that they are okay. Old people are particularly vulnerable to heatwaves.

A: Okay, I'll call them. I'll also get in touch with their neighbors, and ask if they can keep an eye on them.

B: That's a good idea.

Writing

2·47 Write about heatwaves.

Example:

With climate change, there will be more heatwaves than before. They will be hotter and last longer. It is important to prepare for heatwaves. Start by checking your air-conditioning system and fans. Remember to drink a lot of water, and avoid going out when temperatures are high. Keep in contact with your family, friends, and neighbors.

Research question

Which countries are vulnerable to heatwaves?

Check the internet and get information about countries that are
vulnerable to heatwaves.

Example:

The three most vulnerable countries to heatwaves are Qatar, Belgium,
and Luxembourg. Qatar is an extremely hot country located in the Middle
East. But Belgium and Luxembourg have relatively low temperatures in
the summer. These countries are vulnerable because they have an aging
population, many of whom suffer from heart disease. Also, they lack the
infrastructure necessary to cope with heatwaves.

Unit 13

Renewable energy

Coal, petroleum, and natural gas are examples of fossil fuels. They are known as non-renewable energy resources. These sources of energy will not last for ever. It is estimated that the world will run out of oil in 50 years, gas in 70 years, and coal in 250 years. Burning fossil fuels creates greenhouse gases that cause climate change. Continued use of non-renewable energy resources is not sustainable.

Renewable energy resources are known as renewables for short. The main renewables are solar, wind, tidal, wave, geothermal, and hydroelectric. The greatest advantage of renewables is that they have no limits and can be used again and again. Additionally, renewables do not give off any CO_2 emissions, and can be thought of as answers to some of our current environmental problems. Let's look at some examples of renewables, and consider their advantages and disadvantages.

Solar power derives energy from sunlight, which can be stored in solar panels, and converted into electricity. A lot of research has been carried out on solar power because this type of energy supply is limitless. It can be used to power houses and larger buildings, and has other applications. Solar power has massive potential, but issues concerning the cost and efficiency of solar panels remain.

Wind power has a lot of potential. Huge wind turbines have been installed on land and in the sea. These turbines are turned by the power of the wind and create energy that is made into electricity. Making and installing wind turbines is expensive. Some people complain that they look ugly. People who live near wind turbines say that noise is an issue. In some cases, plans for the construction of large wind farms have been opposed by local people.

Tidal energy is created by the movement of seawater. Most tidal energy systems are constructed at the mouth of estuaries. As the water flows in and out with the tide, an underwater turbine is turned and electricity is created. Cost is an issue and not all estuaries are suitable for construction of such systems. Some environmentalists are against the construction of tidal energy systems on the grounds that birds and animals will be negatively affected.

Wave energy comes from the movement of seawater, which is used to compress trapped air to drive a turbine. Such projects are extremely suitable for island countries, and are generally done on a small scale. Construction and maintenance costs, as well as criticism from local inhabitants and environmentalists, are also issues.

Geothermal energy is available in areas that have volcanoes. Geothermal energy systems use the natural heat of the earth by pumping water underground. This becomes steam that can be used to heat homes and buildings. This kind of system is being successfully used in the US, Indonesia, the Philippines, and New Zealand.

As we have seen, renewable energy sources have a lot of potential that will make it possible to reduce our reliance on fossil fuels. As technology improves, more renewable energy resources will become available. However, we should not forget that it is still important to reduce the amount of energy that we use. For example, you can generate your own energy by installing solar panels on the roof of your house. If you insulate your house with foam or fiberglass, it will make it possible to save energy. You can switch to LED bulbs, which save both energy and money. In winter, if you wear an extra layer of clothing, you can turn down the heating and reduce the amount of energy you use. These are just a few of the many ways you can use energy more wisely.

Match the words

Match the words 1 – 13 with the answers a – m.

_____	1. fossil fuel	a.	dependence on
_____	2. run out of	b.	for the reason that
_____	3. sustainable	c.	express dissatisfaction, displeasure, unhappiness
_____	4. derive	d.	changed
_____	5. converted	e.	take/receive/obtain from a specified source
_____	6. application	f.	use, utilization,
_____	7. complain	g.	non-renewable energy resources
_____	8. estuary	h.	can be maintained/supported continuously
_____	9. environmentalist	i.	to use all of something, not have any left
_____	10. on the grounds	j.	to prevent heat loss by using special materials
_____	11. criticism	k.	a person concerned about the environment
_____	12. reliance	l.	the mouth of a river
_____	13. insulate	m.	to find faults or mistakes in something

Answer the questions

Read questions 1 – 16 and choose the best answer from a – p.

Paragraph 1

_____ 1. What are non-renewable energy resources also called?

_____ 2. What does burning fossil fuels create?

Paragraph 2

_____ 3. What are renewable energy resources known as?

_____ 4. What is the biggest advantage of renewables?

Paragraph 3

_____ 5. Where does solar power come from?

_____ 6. What are the problems with solar panels?

Paragraph 4

_____ 7. Where can we find wind turbines?

_____ 8. Who opposed the construction of large wind farms?

Paragraph 5

____ 9. Where are most tidal energy systems constructed?

____ 10. Which group of people is against tidal energy systems?

Paragraph 6

____ 11. What is the best location for wave energy projects?

____ 12. Which groups of people criticized wave energy?

Paragraph 7

____ 13. In what kind of places is geothermal energy available?

____ 14. In geothermal energy, where is the water pumped?

Paragraph 8

____ 15. What is one way of creating your own energy?

____ 16. How can you save both energy and money?

....

a. On land and in the sea

b. Local inhabitants and environmentalists

c. Underground

d. Areas that have volcanoes

e. Environmentalists

f. Putting solar panels on your roof

g. Fossil fuels

h. By changing to LED bulbs

i. Cost and efficiency

j. Renewables

k. Greenhouse gases that cause climate change

l. Sunlight

m. Local people

n. Island countries

o. At the mouth of estuaries

p. They have no limits

Check the facts

Are these statements true (T), false (F), or not given (NG) according to the information in the passage?

Paragraph 1

_____ 1. Fossil fuels are renewable and will last for ever.

_____ 2. Using oil, gas, and coal is responsible for climate change.

Paragraph 2.

_____ 3. Renewable energy resources are limitless.

_____ 4. Renewables need further development before they can be used.

Paragraph 3

_____ 5. Houses and larger buildings can be powered by using solar power.

_____ 6. Some researchers believe that solar power has no future.

Paragraph 4

_____ 7. Wind power has more potential than any other renewable resource.

_____ 8. One criticism is that wind turbines do not look beautiful.

Paragraph 5

_____ 9. Most tidal energy systems are built in the middle of the ocean.

_____ 10. Environmentalists think tidal energy systems will hurt birds and animals.

Paragraph 6

_____ 11. Wave energy technology can only be used in developing countries.

_____ 12. The majority of wave energy projects are done on a huge scale.

Paragraph 7

_____ 13. Geothermal energy systems pump water underground.

_____ 14. Geothermal energy has been successful in a number of different countries.

Paragraph 8

_____ 15. It is still important for people to use energy wisely and reduce consumption.

_____ 16. You can save energy by insulating your home.

Choose the best headings

Paragraph 1

1. Fossil fuels can be used indefinitely
2. Problems with the use of non-renewable energy resources

Paragraph 2

1. The main renewable energy resources
2. Current environmental problems caused by renewables

Paragraph 3

1. We need to overcome the disadvantages of solar power
2. The potential of solar power is enormous

Paragraph 4

1. There are several issues with wind power such as cost and noise
2. Local people are aware of the advantages of wind power

Paragraph 5

1. Tidal energy systems can be built in most but not all estuaries
2. There are no issues at all with tidal energy systems

Paragraph 6

1. Wave energy projects can be used all over the world in every situation
2. Wave energy projects were opposed by local people and environmentalists

Paragraph 7

1. Volcanic areas have geothermal energy potential
2. Geothermal energy projects are possible in all countries

Paragraph 8

1. Even though renewables have potential, we should continue to reduce our energy use
2. Solar panels, insulation, and LED bulbs have little effect

Speaking

Talk about renewable energy.

A: What are renewables?

B: They are renewable energy resources. The main ones are solar, wind, tidal, wave, geothermal, and hydroelectric.

A: Why do we need renewables?

B: Because fossil fuels such as coal, petroleum, and natural gas will not last forever. That's one problem. Another problem is that burning these fuels causes global warming.

A: I have heard a lot about solar power recently. Doesn't it have some serious problems?

B: The good point about solar power is that it is limitless. It means it never runs out. It has massive potential. But there are some issues. Some people say that solar panels cost too much and are inefficient.

A: Are there any solutions to those problems?

B: Researchers are still working on those issues and, in the long-term, they should be able to overcome them. I am very optimistic about solar power.

Writing

Write about renewable energy.

Example:

Continued use of fossil fuels creates greenhouse gases that cause climate change. It is important to focus on renewable energy. Solar power has a lot of potential. Today many houses and other buildings have solar panels on their roofs and walls. Additionally, solar power plants, which are also known as solar panel farms, are becoming more common.

Research question

Which countries generate the most solar power?

Check the Internet and get information about which countries generate the most solar power.

Example:

The top four countries for generating solar power are China, the United States, India, and Japan. After the Fukushima nuclear plant disaster in 2011, Japan put a lot of emphasis on solar power, and announced a plan to double this type of renewable energy by 2030. Japan's solar energy technology is improving rapidly. Floating water-resistant solar panels have been developed and are being used on lakes and reservoirs in Japan.

Unit 14

Smart Cities

The first cities to start using computer systems for management and development were Los Angeles in the late 1960's and Singapore in 1981. In 2011, a Smart City Expo World Congress took place in Barcelona. Following that, Chinese cities took the lead in developing smart cities. Now, around 50 percent of the world's smart cities are located in China. The number of smart cities is increasing and by 2050 as many as 75 percent of the world's population will be living in such cities.

Smart cities are modern urban areas that are technologically advanced. They make use of data on citizens, buildings and other things, that are collected by electronic methods, and sensors. Information derived from that data is employed to manage resources and services. The goal of a smart city is to enhance operations throughout the city. Smart city technology can improve important quality of life indicators such as health, environment, and safety by between 10 to 30 percent.

Smart cities have numerous advantages. First, transportation. Smart cities have electric vehicles as well as vehicles that run on hydrogen energy. Second, residents of smart cities can enjoy a high degree of safety. Through the use of advanced equipment and monitoring systems, smart cities are much safer than the average city. Sensors, CCTV cameras, and other devices are positioned in shopping malls, stations, parks, and other places. Third, sustainability. Currently, most cities rely on energy sources that will run out, such as oil, coal, and natural gas. Smart cities generate electricity by solar and wind power, as well as other renewable resources. This energy efficient infrastructure improves air quality. The most commonly mentioned disadvantage of smart cities is limited privacy. Smart cities are full of CCTV cameras and other monitoring devices that are used to gather data. Some people fear that their privacy can be invaded easily. Another issue is the fact that the system depends too heavily on the internet. A small problem with the system could cause huge problems that would affect people at home and at work, and when they are making a journey. The last issue is cybercrime. If hackers get into the system, sensitive data can be stolen.

In Japan, some major companies are involved in the development of smart cities. Take, for example, Fujisawa City in Kanagawa, which was built by Panasonic, a world-famous company for manufacturing electronic appliances. The city is known as Fujisawa Sustainable Smart Town. It is supported by several businesses, universities, local governments, and other organizations. It opened in 2014 and was scheduled for completion in 2022. It focused on energy, security, transport, health, and community. Some of the major targets were to reduce CO_2 emissions by 70 percent, cut consumption of water by 30 percent, and have renewable energy make up 30 percent of all energy used.

Another important smart city in Japan is Woven City, Mount Fuji. The city is backed by Toyota and is being constructed at a former vehicle production factory. It is being built from scratch. Although the project is on a small scale, the fact that it is being done from zero provides a perfect opportunity to develop and test future technologies. Hydrogen fuel cells will be used to produce clean energy that will power cars, homes, and businesses. Buildings will be hi-tech. Photo-voltaic panels that generate solar power will be installed on the roofs of all buildings. Streets will be divided into three types for use by fast vehicles, slow vehicles, and pedestrians. Technologies such as robotics, smart homes, and AI will be tested.

Many cities around the world are adopting the technology that is being developed in smart cities in Japan. Global spending on creating and developing smart cities reached about 125 billion US dollars in 2020. The fastest growth in spending on smart cities is predicted to be in Japan and Latin America. Smart cities will provide advantages to people all over the world by improving quality of life, creating sustainability, and smart use of resources.

Match the words

Match the words 1 – 11 with the answers a – k.

_____ 1. smart city
_____ 2. congress
_____ 3. derived from
_____ 4. employed
_____ 5. enhance
_____ 6. indicators
_____ 7. infrastructure
_____ 8. cybercrime
_____ 9. former
_____ 10. from scratch
_____ 11. adopting

a. used
b. improve
c. buildings, roads, bridges and so on
d. a thing that indicates the level of something
e. previous
f. from zero
g. taken from, originate from,
h. meeting, conference
i. modern urban area that is technologically
   advanced
j. selecting, choosing, using
k. crime carried out using computers or the internet

Answer the questions

Read questions 1 – 12 and choose the best answer from a – l.

Paragraph 1

_____ 1. Currently, how many of the world's smart cities are in China?

_____ 2. What percentage of the world's population will be living in smart cities by 2050?

Paragraph 2

_____ 3. How is data collected?

_____ 4. By how much does smart city technology improve quality of life?

Paragraph 3.

_____ 5. What do vehicles in smart cities run on?

_____ 6. What is the most significant demerit of living in a smart city?

Paragraph 4

_____ 7. By how much did Fujisawa City want to cut CO2 emissions?

_____ 8. By how much did Fujisawa City want to cut water consumption?

Paragraph 5

_____ 9. Which company is supporting the construction of Woven City, Mount Fuji?

_____ 10. What will be on the roofs of buildings?

Paragraph 6

_____ 11. What do we know about technology that is being developed in smart cities in Japan?

_____ 12. Where will the growth in spending on smart cities be fastest?

a. As many as 75 percent

b. Toyota

c. Limited privacy

d. By 70 percent

e. By 30 percent

f. Between 10 to 30 percent

g. It is being used by many cities all over the world

h. Electricity and hydrogen energy

i. Japan and Latin America

j. By electronic methods and sensors

k. Around 50 percent

l. Photo-voltaic panels

Check the facts

Are these statements true (T), false (F), or not given (NG) according to the information in the passage?

Paragraph 1

_____ 1. China's development of smart cities preceded the Smart City Expo World Congress.

_____ 2. China is currently exporting smart city technology.

Paragraph 2

_____ 3. Smart cities are being planned in predominantly rural areas.

_____ 4. Data collected in smart cities are applied to management of resources and services.

Paragraph 3

_____ 5. Levels of safety in smart cities exceed those commonly found in standard cities.

_____ 6. Sensors and cameras are used in smart cities to catch criminals.

Paragraph 4

_____ 7. Smart cities use renewable energy resources.

_____ 8. Smart cities manufacture CCTV cameras.

Paragraph 5

_____ 9. Woven City is being constructed on a site that was previously a car factory.

_____ 10. Streets in the city are divided into 2 main types.

Paragraph 6

_____ 11. Spending on creating and developing smart cities around the world was about 125 billion USD in 2020.

_____ 12. Developing countries have plans to create and develop smart cities.

Choose the best headings

Paragraph 1

1. Governments are planning new smart cities all over the world
2. How smart cities started and developed

Paragraph 2

1. Smart city technology can be used to enhance quality of life indicators
2. Smart city technology has no effects on the health of residents

Paragraph 3

1. Advantages of smart cities include transportation, safety, and renewable resources
2. The system is good but there is a chance of data being stolen

Paragraph 4

1. Fujisawa City is responsible for developing new businesses for people
2. Fujisawa City receives support from a number of different sources

Paragraph 5

1. Woven City is a small-scale smart city project that started from zero
2. In Woven City, pedestrians share streets with fast and slow vehicles

Paragraph 6

1. Japan is importing smart city technology
2. Japan and Latin America are predicted to lead spending on smart cities

Speaking

Talk about smart cities.

A: The term 'smart city' keeps coming up in the news. Do you know what it means?

B: It refers to cities that use information and communication technology to improve the city and quality of life of people who live there.

A: What does that mean exactly? It is difficult to imagine how it works.

B: It means that cities collect data using sensors. For example, they monitor the flow of traffic in the city. The data are stored, analyzed, and used to improve roads, traffic signals, and different types of transportation.

A: Is that all?

B: No, the next step is to analyze the data to improve the quality of life of residents.

A: Are there any other examples?

B: Basically, smart cities use technology such as autonomy, robotics, mobility, smart homes, and AI to improve the economy, city, and lives of the inhabitants.

Writing

Write about smart cities.

Example:

By 2050, almost 75 percent of the world's population will be living in smart cities. These cities have several advantages that improve the lives of residents. Cars, buses, and trucks will run on hydrogen energy. The use of cameras and sensors will make smart cities safe places to live. Clean energy will be generated by renewable energy resources such as solar and wind power.

....

....

Research question

Why are smart cities important?

Check the internet and get information about why smart cities are important.

Example:

The world's population is increasing and more people are moving to cities. Governments need to take action to ensure sustainable development in cities. Smart cities are important because they have advanced technologies that will improve the infrastructure in cities, and make it possible to carry out effective planning and decision making. Transportation will be improved, and communities will be safer.

Improving Academic English

検印 省略	©2023 年 1 月 31 日　第 1 版発行

著　者　　　　　　　　　Clive Langham

発行者　　　　　　　　　小川　洋一郎

発売所　　　　　　　　　株式会社 朝日出版社

101-0065　東京都千代田区西神田 3-3-5
電話（03）3239-0271
FAX（03）3239-0479
e-mail: text-e@asahipress.com
振替口座　00140-2-46008
組版・Office haru ／製版・錦明印刷

乱丁、落丁本はお取り替えいたします
ISBN 978-4-255-15702-3 C1082

就活・留学準備の強力な味方!

あなたのグローバル英語力を測定

新時代のオンラインテスト

CNN GLENTS

留学・就活により役立つ新時代のオンラインテストCNN GLENTSが誕生! CNNの生きた英語を使った新しい英語力測定テストがいよいよ始まりました! 詳しくはCNN GLENTSホームページをご覧ください。

https://www.asahipress.com/special/glents

CNN GLENTSとは

GLENTSとは、**GLobal ENglish Testing System**という名の通り、世界標準の英語力を測るシステムです。リアルな英語を聞き取るリスニングセクション、海外の話題を読み取るリーディングセクション、異文化を理解するのに必要な知識を問う国際教養セクションから構成される、世界に通じる「ホンモノ」の英語力を測定するためのテストです。

CNN GLENTSの特長

■作られた英語ではなく生の英語ニュースが素材
リスニング問題、リーディング問題、いずれも世界最大のニュース専門放送局CNNの英語ニュースから出題。実際のニュース映像を使った「動画視聴問題」も導入しています。

■場所を選ばず受験できるオンライン方式
コンピューターやスマートフォン、タブレットなどの端末とインターネット接続があれば、好きな場所で受けられます。

■自動採点で結果をすぐに表示　国際指標CEFRにも対応
テスト終了後、自動採点ですぐに結果がわかります。国際的な評価基準であるCEFRとの対照レベルやTOEIC®Listening & Reading Testの予測スコアも表示されます。

■コミュニケーションに必要な社会・文化知識にも配慮
独自のセクションとして設けた「国際教養セクション」では、

世界で活躍する人材に求められる異文化理解力を測ります。

■試験時間は約70分、受験料は¥3,960円(税込)です。

※画像はイメージです。

お問い合わせ先　株式会社 朝日出版社　「CNN GLENTS」事務局
フリーダイヤル: **0120-181-202**　E-MAIL: **glents_support@asahipress.com**
(平日午前10時〜午後6時)